AMERICA the BEAUTIFUL
ALABAMA

By Sylvia McNair

Consultants

Elizabeth C. Garrison, Elementary Curriculum Specialist, Talladega City Schools, Talladega, Alabama

Mary B. Grant, Teacher, Collegeview Elementary School, Troy, Alabama; former Consultant for the Alabama Department of Education

Robert L. Hillerich, Ph.D., Bowling Green State University, Bowling Green, Ohio

CHILDRENS PRESS ®
CHICAGO

A pond at Jasmine Hill near Wetumpka in Elmore County

Project Editor: Joan Downing
Assistant Editor: Shari Joffe
Design Director: Margrit Fiddle
Typesetting: Graphic Connections, Inc.
Engraving: Liberty Photoengraving

Childrens Press®, Chicago
Copyright ©1989 by Regensteiner Publishing Enterprises, Inc.
All rights reserved. Published simultaneously in Canada.
Printed in the United States of America.
1 2 3 4 5 6 7 8 9 10 R 98 97 96 95 94 93 92 91 90 89

Library of Congress Cataloging-in-Publication Data

McNair, Sylvia.
 . America the beautiful. Alabama / by Sylvia McNair.
     p.   cm.
   Includes index:
   Summary: Introduces the geography, history,
government, economy, industry, culture, historic sites, and
famous people of this southern state.
   ISBN 0-516-00447-6
   1.   Alabama—Juvenile
literature. [1.   Alabama.]   I.   Title.
F326.3.M34   1988   88-11744
976.1—dc19   CIP
                                                    AC

Riverchase Galleria,
a popular Birmingham
shopping mall

TABLE OF CONTENTS

Chapter 1

STARS FELL ON ALABAMA

STARS FELL ON ALABAMA

More than 150 years ago, in 1833, nature treated Alabama to a spectacular fireworks show—a meteor shower. For years afterward, parents and grandparents told their children about the unusual and exciting event. A hundred years later, a popular song, "Stars Fell on Alabama," was even written.

Nature has bestowed a number of other gifts on this southern state: the longest natural rock bridge in the eastern United States; the deepest gorge east of the Mississippi River; a spectacular cavern, Russell Cave, where prehistoric people lived more than eight thousand years ago. Alabama boasts beautiful scenery and plenty of opportunities for outdoor recreation. Forests cover two-thirds of the state, and rivers and lakes furnish about a million acres (.4 million hectares) of water for swimming, boating, waterskiing, and fishing.

Alabama's history is full of contrasts. Its southern strip, bordered by the Gulf of Mexico, was settled by French and Spanish explorers. The rest of the state was settled largely by people of Anglo-Saxon descent.

One of Alabama's nicknames is the "Heart of Dixie." Montgomery, the state's capital, is called the "Cradle of the Confederacy" because it was the first capital of the Confederate States of America during the Civil War. Montgomery is also known as the birthplace of the Civil Rights Movement of the 1960s.

But these are only a few of the facts that make Alabama such an interesting state. Let's take a look, now, at this state where the stars once fell.

Chapter 2
THE LAND

THE LAND

The land of Alabama slopes gently downward from the northeastern third of the state to the coastal plains in the south. If you raised one corner of a card table a few inches, you'd get an idea of how the whole state seems to slant toward the short coastline of the Gulf of Mexico at the southwest corner of the state.

Alabama is bounded by Tennessee on the north, Georgia on the east, Florida and the Gulf of Mexico on the south, and Mississippi on the west. It covers 51,705 square miles (133,915 square kilometers), and ranks twenty-ninth in size among the fifty states.

TOPOGRAPHY

Geographers divide Alabama into six land regions. The Interior Low Plateau lies in the northwest. The Cumberland Plateau extends like a finger from the northeast corner toward the center of the state. The Appalachian Ridge and Valley Region covers the area southeast of and parallel to the Cumberland Plateau. Southeast of the Appalachian Region is a triangular region known as the Piedmont. The East Gulf Coastal Plain covers approximately the southern one-third of the state. The Black Belt is the name for the narrow strip of fertile bottomland that slices into the East Gulf Coastal Plain.

Noccalula Falls
in northeastern
Alabama

FROM NORTH TO SOUTH

Rolling land, woods, and lakes give variety and beauty to the northern plateaus. The mountains of the Appalachian Ridge and Valley and Piedmont regions are low, but wooded and picturesque. The highest mountain in the state, Cheaha Mountain, stands only 2,407 feet (734 meters) above sea level.

Waterfalls cascade down the mountain slopes. Cold mountain streams cut gorges and canyons into the landscape. Wildflowers color the hillsides with violet, scarlet, yellow, and pink in spring and summer; autumn leaves paint the hills with even brighter

Northern Alabama offers breathtaking scenery.

colors each fall. Underground caves form huge rooms with varicolored ceilings. Lakes of every size—from modest mountain pools to huge, deep, man-made reservoirs—sparkle in the sunshine.

South of the mountainous regions are low hills covered with pine forests. The soil here is full of sand and gravel. Still sloping downward, the land eventually becomes swampy, until it ends at Mobile Bay and the sandy shores and barrier islands of the Gulf of Mexico.

Just south of the center of the state, another type of land is found. This is the Black Belt, a 25-to-50-mile- (40-to-80-kilometer-) wide strip of rich bottomland that stretches across central

A lush woodland near Sipsey in the north-central part of the state

Mississippi and Alabama. The fertile black soil here is quite different from the tan and red earth common in much of the southeastern United States. The largest and most productive plantations of the pre-Civil War days were located in the Black Belt, and the area still contains some of the best agricultural land in the region.

Alabama's coastline is only 53 miles (85 kilometers) long. The state has two large bays: Mobile and Perdido. Mobile Bay has an excellent harbor. The United States Army Corps of Engineers has dredged the deep-water channel into the bay several times so that oceangoing vessels can come into port. Perdido Bay, on the border between Alabama and Florida, is edged by semitropical swamplands.

The Mobile River delta area covers about 400 square miles (1,036 square kilometers) of marshes and cypress swamps that are home to alligators, fish, and many kinds of waterfowl. Dauphin

Gulf Shores, at Alabama's southeastern tip, reaches into the Gulf of Mexico.

Island, a 30-mile- (48-kilometer-) long barrier island south of Mobile, is a popular recreational area. It was first discovered and mapped in the sixteenth century by Spanish explorers.

RIVERS AND LAKES

Rivers have been important in Alabama's history ever since the first European explorers paddled up the Mobile and Alabama rivers from the Gulf of Mexico. In the twentieth century, these rivers have become more important than ever. Giant dams have been constructed to harness their waterpower and to create beautiful lakes.

The Tennessee River cuts a loop across the northern part of the state from the northeast to the northwest corner. Principal rivers in the east are the Coosa, the Callapoosa, and the Chattahoochee. The Alabama and the Tombigbee meet to form the Mobile River,

The locks at
Wilson Dam on the
Tennessee River

which flows into Mobile Bay. A major water project that was
completed recently by the states of Mississippi and Alabama is the
Tennessee-Tombigbee Waterway, which connects the Tennessee
and Tombigbee rivers and provides a route from the Tennessee
River to Mobile Bay.

Dams on the Tennessee River have formed Pickwick, Wilson,
Wheeler, and Guntersville lakes. The Coosa River has been
dammed to create Weiss Lake, Logan Martin Lake, and Lake
Mitchell. On the Chattahoochee River along the Georgia-Alabama
border are West Point Lake, most of which lies in Georgia; Lake
Harding; and Lake Eufaula. Martin Lake lies on the Tallapoosa
River.

Besides its major rivers, Alabama has many smaller streams and
rivers that are popular for fishing and canoeing. Generally,
southern Alabama rivers are slower and have fewer rocks and
rapids than those in northern Alabama. The Cahaba River, which
begins near Birmingham and flows to Selma, is called "Alabama's
most floated river." Alabamians and other visitors enjoy hiking,
observing wildlife, and visiting historic and archaeological sites
along its shores. The Blackwater, which flows into the Perdido

Guntersville Lake, formed by a dam on the Tennessee River, is Alabama's largest lake.

near the western edge of Florida, is a crystal-clear, spring-fed river with bluffs, rapids, white sandy banks, and cypress stands. The state has specially designated an 11-mile (18-kilometer) stretch of the Little River in the northeastern part of the state as a Wild and Scenic River.

CLIMATE

Although Alabama's climate is generally mild, it varies slightly from region to region. The lower coastal plain is largely subtropical, while temperatures in the northern plateaus can drop low enough to allow snowfall in winter. In the Black Belt and the upper coastal plain, temperatures fall somewhere between these two extremes.

The mild climate and fertile soil of Alabama's Black Belt region make it ideal for growing crops.

Summers in Alabama are generally hot; July temperatures average about 80 degrees Fahrenheit (27 degrees Celsius). In winter, temperatures average about 46 degrees Fahrenheit (8 degrees Celsius) in the northern part of the state and about 52 degrees Fahrenheit (11 degrees Celsius) in the south. On an average winter afternoon along the coast, the temperature climbs into the low sixties.

Rainfall is abundant in all parts of the state throughout the year. Average annual precipitation ranges from about 53 inches (135 centimeters) in northern Alabama to 65 inches (165 centimeters) along the coast. Occasionally, hurricanes sweep across the Gulf of Mexico and cause damage to areas near the shore. However, residents usually have sufficient warning of coming storms to be able to find temporary safe shelter.

Chapter 3
THE PEOPLE

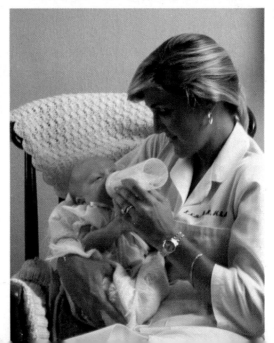

THE PEOPLE

The region now known as the state of Alabama has been inhabited for thousands of years. When Europeans first explored the area, they encountered four major Native American groups— Creeks, Chickasaws, Choctaws, and Cherokees. Ancestors of these people had lived in Alabama for at least eight thousand years.

Today, fewer than eight thousand descendants of these Native Americans remain in Alabama. A few Creeks live in southern Alabama, and some Cherokees live in the northeastern corner of the state.

ALABAMA'S ETHNIC HERITAGE

Most of Alabama's people are descended from either Anglo-Saxon or African forebears. Mobile, however, was settled by the French and was ruled for a time by the Spanish, and the atmosphere of this port city is still somewhat Latin. Like New Orleans, Mobile is a city where people enjoy fashion, fine food, parties, and high society. The city's Latin heritage is especially evident during the Mardi Gras season.

Although Mobile's earliest citizens were from France and Spain, Americans and other immigrants began to settle there after the United States seized the region from Spain in 1813. Before the Civil War, about one thousand free blacks lived in Mobile. As Alabama's only port city, Mobile had more exposure to people from other parts of the world than did the rest of the state. In the

At Bellingrath Gardens, tour guides dressed as southern belles remind visitors of Alabama's colorful antebellum era.

1880s, a national magazine reported that Mobile's population was more varied in nationality and descent than that of any other American city. Although this was undoubtedly an exaggeration, it does emphasize Mobile's diversity.

In the mid-1800s, Irish, Scottish, German, and Italian immigrants began coming to Alabama to work in the coal mines and iron furnaces around Birmingham. Scandinavians, Italians, Greeks, and other Europeans settled in Baldwin County, across the bay from Mobile, in the late 1800s and early 1900s.

A German immigrant named Colonel Johann Cullman founded a town in north-central Alabama in 1873. Wishing to build a strong colony for German immigrants, he brought in several thousand people to work on farms and establish small businesses. Although the people of Cullman originally held on to the language and culture of their homeland, they eventually assimilated into the general population.

Most Alabamians belong to one of two ethnic groups. The majority of white Alabamians are of English or Scotch-Irish ancestry; most black Alabamians are descended from African slaves. Blacks make up about one-fourth of the total population. In 1860, nearly half of the state's residents were black. After the Civil War, many blacks moved away from the state. Another exodus of blacks took place during World War II, as people sought jobs in northern cities. In recent years, as blacks have begun to make economic and social gains in Alabama, this trend has been reversed.

Only a few people of Asian ancestry live in the state, and only about 1 percent of Alabama's nearly 4 million people are foreign-born.

POPULATION DISTRIBUTION

The 1980 census reported that a total of 3,893,978 people live in Alabama, making it twenty-second in population among the states.

Three out of five Alabamians live in urban areas. One-fifth of the people live in one of the four largest cities—Birmingham, Mobile, Montgomery, and Huntsville.

Population density varies widely in the state, from a low of 16.4 people per square mile (6.3 people per square kilometer) in Coosa County, in the center of the state; to a high of 578.5 people per square mile (223.4 people per square kilometer) in Jefferson County, which includes Birmingham.

RELIGION

In the days of the early French settlers, and then again when Alabama came under Spanish rule in the late 1700s, Roman Catholicism was the official religion of the region. The first Baptist church in Alabama was organized in 1808.

A United Methodist
church in Russell County

Churches were very important during the frontier days. They served as community centers or social gathering places. People went to church not just to worship, but also to gather news and information, to see friends, and to sing and play instruments. A community's rules of conduct were set by the church. Early Baptists and Methodists demanded strict obedience to these rules. Members were expelled for such sins as betting, dancing, or drinking.

Most slaveholders forced their slaves to go to church, where they were seated in the back pews. After the Civil War, blacks began to form their own churches, led by black pastors. Black preachers became important community leaders, and they still occupy positions of great influence. Black churches encouraged education; classes were held to teach former slaves to read and write.

Today, Baptists represent the largest single religious group in the state. About one-fourth of the state's residents belong to the Southern Baptist Church. The United Methodist Church and the Churches of Christ have the second- and third-largest number of followers. Episcopalians, Presbyterians, and Roman Catholics also reside in Alabama, and the state has a tiny Jewish population. About one hundred thousand Roman Catholics and ten thousand Jews live in the state.

Chapter 4

THE BEGINNING

THE BEGINNING

The first Europeans to spot the coast of what is now the state of Alabama were Spanish sailors with vivid imaginations. Just a few years after Columbus first sailed to the New World—perhaps as early as 1505—tales were being told of a land where "the people wear hats of solid gold and life is gay and luxurious."

PREHISTORIC ALABAMIANS

Thousands of years ago, cliff-dwelling people lived in the northern part of what is now Alabama. Archaeologists have found evidence that Russell Cave, in northeastern Alabama, was used for shelter as early as 7000 B.C., and perhaps even as early as ten thousand years ago. These early people were hunters who used the cave as a camping place in fall and winter. Tools and other discarded items found on the floor of the cave show that it was used by many generations. Much later, around A.D. 1000, farming began to replace hunting, and visits to the cave became less frequent.

Shards of pottery made about four thousand years ago have been found along the Tennessee River in northern Alabama.

South of Tuscaloosa is a town called Moundville, named for the forty-odd burial mounds built there about eight hundred years ago. At that time, between nine thousand and thirteen thousand people inhabited the site. The largest mound covers nearly 2 acres (.8 hectares) and is 58 feet (18 meters) high. Artifacts uncovered at

Mound State Monument near Moundville preserves the artifacts (above) and ceremonial mounds (right) of an Indian group that inhabited the site about eight hundred years ago.

the site indicate that the Moundville people knew how to make fine pottery, stone carvings, and copper ornaments.

When European settlers first came to the Alabama region, they encountered people of two Native American (American Indian) groups: the Creek, Choctaw, and Chickasaw tribes of the Muskhogean people; and the Cherokees, who were an Iroquoian people. These four groups, along with the Seminoles of Florida, were later called the Five Civilized Tribes by the United States Bureau of Indian Affairs. White people considered them "civilized" because they adopted the customs of the European settlers more readily than most other tribes on the continent— especially in the areas of government and education. Their society was primarily agricultural. They raised corn, beans, tobacco, and squash, and lived in log houses. Some of them became Christians, and some even intermarried with the colonists.

SPANISH EXPLORATION

In 1539, Spanish explorer Hernando De Soto sailed from Cuba to the coast of the Gulf of Mexico. Two years earlier, De Soto had been appointed governor of Cuba by the king of Spain. A royal patent granted him rights to "all lands on the north of Florida over which he shall extend the sovereignty of his Catholic Majesty, Charles V.''

De Soto and his six hundred men did not enter Alabama from the coast. They landed near present-day Tampa Bay, Florida, and wandered north, probably traveling as far as the Smoky Mountains. From there they turned south and west, entering Alabama from the northeast. De Soto and his men were ruthless invaders. During a battle at the Indian village of Mabila in southwestern Alabama, they slaughtered thousands of Indians.

No settlements resulted from this earliest expedition into the interior of Alabama. The Spanish attempted to found a colony near Mobile Bay in 1559, but it was not successful. Spanish explorer Tristan de Luna and a thousand colonists had been sent to the region from Mexico to search for gold, but after three years of looking in vain, they abandoned the territory and returned to Mexico.

The coast of Alabama remained unsettled for more than a hundred years. It was considered a part of Florida, first claimed by Spain and later by England and France.

FRENCH SETTLEMENT

In 1698, King Louis XIV of France sent Pierre Le Moyne, Sieur d'Iberville, and his brother, Jean Baptiste Le Moyne, Sieur de Bienville, to establish a settlement on the Gulf coast. Near the site of present-day Ocean Springs, Mississippi, the brothers founded the first capital of the huge Louisiana territory claimed by France. In 1702, they moved the capital to a bluff near the Mobile River and named it Fort Louis de la Mobile.

Iberville, now governor of French Louisiana, wanted Fort Louis to be a permanent settlement, so he imported orphan girls to marry the male colonists. The young women were called "cassette girls" because the government had given each bride a *cassette* (the French word for trunk) and an outfit of clothing.

After a flood in 1711, the capital was moved to the site of present-day Mobile, where it was again called Fort Louis. Renamed Fort Conde de la Mobile in 1720, it remained the capital of French Louisiana until 1722.

The early colonists were a curious mix of French Canadian fur traders, unambitious vagrants, criminals, and down-on-their-luck gentlemen. Although the colony grew slowly to a population of about six thousand, the government of France gave it little support. On at least one occasion, the settlers nearly starved because supply ships expected from home did not arrive.

France had to give up its North American possessions as a result of its defeat in the French and Indian War. The terms of the Treaty of Paris, signed in 1763, gave Canada and all French possessions east of the Mississippi River (including all of present-day Alabama) to Great Britain, and gave the lands west of the Mississippi to Spain.

AFTER THE REVOLUTION

At the end of the American Revolution, in 1783, Great Britain agreed to give much of northern Alabama, then part of Georgia, to the United States. The Mobile region was at that time part of Florida, which was ceded to Spain. In 1798, Congress made northern Alabama a part of the Territory of Mississippi, and appointed William C. C. Claiborne as territorial governor.

Napoleon of France pressured Spain to return the Louisiana territory to France in 1800, then sold it to the United States in 1803. Mobile's status was not clear. The United States claimed it

Chief Menewa (above) was one of the Creek Indians defeated by Andrew Jackson's troops at Horseshoe Bend (left), shown as it appears today.

was part of the Louisiana Purchase territory; Spain considered it part of Florida. The conflict was finally resolved when the United States captured the region from Spain during the War of 1812.

In 1813, Creek Indians raided Fort Mims, a few miles north of Mobile near the Alabama River, in an attempt to resist the encroachment of the white colonists. Several hundred settlers were captured and killed. General Andrew Jackson organized the Tennessee militia in a campaign against the Indians. He led his troops in successful battles at Talladega and Horseshoe Bend. His fame as a military leader spread, and his early exploits in Alabama helped him along a career path that eventually led to the presidency.

In 1814, the defeated Creek Indians gave up their land—a territory that amounted to nearly half of present-day Alabama. Congress organized the territory of Alabama in 1817. Two years later, a state constitutional convention was held in Huntsville. On December 14, 1819, Alabama was admitted to the Union as the twenty-second state. Huntsville became the state's first capital.

Chapter 5
CRADLE OF THE CONFEDERACY

PICKING

CRADLE OF THE CONFEDERACY

The new state of Alabama grew rapidly. During the first ten years of statehood, the population doubled, growing from fewer than 128,000 people to more than 300,000.

KING COTTON

Cotton quickly became the most important crop in the state. Slaves had first been brought into the region in 1719, and as the cotton industry grew, the South became increasingly dependent on slavery.

Early methods of growing cotton required many field workers to plant and harvest the crop by hand. Cotton fibers grow inside a pod, or boll, which opens up when the plant is ripe. The seeds of the plant are also inside the boll, and the cotton fiber must be separated from both the boll and the seeds. This was a slow, painstaking process that originally had to be done by hand. Then, in 1793, Eli Whitney invented a machine that separated the seeds from the fiber. Whitney's cotton gin made it possible for one person to do as much work as fifty could do by hand. Even so, many workers were still needed to harvest the crops. Slave labor, cotton gins, fertile soil, and steamboat transportation on the Alabama River between Mobile and the cotton plantations in central Alabama made mass production of cotton possible. Stagecoach service soon connected Montgomery, in central Alabama, with the cities of Nashville, Tennessee, and Columbus,

Cotton being loaded
onto a steamboat
on the Alabama
River in the 1850s

Georgia. All these factors, plus fertile soil, turned the Black Belt in
central Alabama into a prosperous agricultural region by the
1820s.

Montgomery and Decatur became lively, growing cities.
Northern Alabama began to develop as well. Huntsville, located
on a stagecoach route between southern Alabama and the
Tennessee River Valley, was a social and commercial center for
the northern region.

Meanwhile, more and more land was being acquired from the
Creek, Chickasaw, Cherokee, and Choctaw Indians through
treaties that always favored the white settlers. In 1838, federal
troops marched into the remaining Indian territory in northern
Alabama and informed the Indians that they would have to move
west of the Mississippi River. Thousands of marchers died along
the difficult route westward, which became known as the Trail of
Tears.

The capital of Alabama was moved several times. The first move
was from Huntsville to Cahaba, in south-central Alabama, in
1820. Although Cahaba was a flourishing town, it was the victim
of periodic floods, and in 1826 the capital was moved to

Montgomery as it appeared in the mid-1800s

Tuscaloosa. Finally, in 1847, a new capitol building was erected in Montgomery, and Montgomery has been the seat of Alabama's government ever since.

SLAVERY AND POLITICS

In the mid-1800s, a number of events began leading the nation toward a civil war. Many reasons have been given to explain why this tragic split between the North and the South occurred. The two most important reasons were conflicts over the issues of slavery and states' rights. Economics played a role as well.

The North was more industrialized than the South. Slaves were not needed in the cities or on the small farms of the North, as they were on southern plantations. Also, many northerners believed that slavery was morally wrong.

Although two-thirds of white Alabamians did not own slaves, most of the political power in the state was held by a small number of wealthy, slaveholding plantation owners. Slavery was essential to the plantation system. Besides, the plantations were a market for the produce raised by small farmers. The entire economy of the state depended on cotton; almost all manufactured goods were purchased from Europe and from the North. Congress levied protective tariffs on certain manufactured goods. These tariffs benefited the North, but made goods very expensive in the South.

Then, as war began to seem inevitable, the final question was one of loyalty. Should a person's loyalty be greater to his own state or to the nation?

Today, most Americans identify more strongly with their country than with their state. Many Americans move from one state to another without any thought that they are changing their citizenship. In the mid-1800s, however, the United States was still quite young. Some people regarded the federal government as simply a voluntary association of several sovereign states, each of which should be allowed to make its own laws without interference. Since they belonged to the federation voluntarily, some southerners reasoned, they should be able to withdraw voluntarily, too—to secede from the Union.

One of Alabama's first two United States senators was Democrat William Rufus King. King worked diligently to settle

As a senator in the early 1800s, Alabamian William Rufus King (left) worked to resolve the differences between the northern and southern states. However, after the election of Abraham Lincoln in 1861, the southern states met in Montgomery to form the Confederate States of America. Jefferson Davis (right) was elected president of the new nation, and Montgomery was declared the capital.

the differences between the slave and free states. In 1852, he was elected vice-president of the United States, the highest political office ever held by an Alabamian. As a strong supporter of the federal government, Vice-President King would undoubtedly have tried to work toward preventing civil war. Unfortunately, he had tuberculosis, and died after only six weeks in office.

WAR BETWEEN THE STATES

The presidential election of 1860 was the spark that touched off the fire. Abraham Lincoln was elected on an antislavery Republican party platform that upset many southerners.

South Carolina was the first state to secede from the Union, and before Lincoln was inaugurated, Mississippi, Florida, Alabama, Georgia, Louisiana, and Texas followed South Carolina's lead. In February 1861, six of the seven states met in Montgomery to form a new nation, the Confederate States of America. Jefferson Davis was elected president, Alexander Stephens was chosen as vice-president, and Montgomery was declared the capital. Because it was the first capital of the Confederacy, Montgomery became

On February 18, 1861, Montgomery's citizens gathered in front of the State Capitol to watch the inauguration of Jefferson Davis as president of the Confederate States of America.

known as the "Cradle of the Confederacy." However, less than four months later, the Confederate Congress voted to move its capital to Richmond, Virginia. Though many Alabamians were disappointed about losing the Confederate capital, one result was that Alabama never became a prime battleground of the war.

As in other mountainous areas of the South, northern Alabama had many residents who were antislavery and pro-Union. Some of these people discussed the possibility of setting up a new pro-Union state, to be called Nickajack. Citizens of Winston County, most of whom were loyal to the Union, actually seceded from the state and declared the county to be the "Free State of Winston." But once the war actually started, the pro-Union movement died

The 1864 Battle of Mobile Bay was the most important Civil War engagement to occur in Alabama.

out, swept away by a tide of patriotism for Alabama and the Confederacy.

It is estimated that about 122,000 Alabamians went to war. About 10,000 blacks and 2,500 whites joined the Union army. Between 8,000 and 10,000 men hid, deserted from the Confederate army, or worked covertly to assist the Union forces.

By 1862, Union forces had invaded Alabama and occupied Huntsville, Decatur, and Tuscumbia. However, Alabama did not suffer as much destruction during the war as did many other southern states, and few battles were fought on Alabama soil. The

Fort Morgan, shown here as it appears today, was one of the forts from which Confederate forces tried to defend Mobile Bay.

most important Civil War engagement in the state was the Battle of Mobile Bay, one of the fiercest naval battles of the war.

The Confederates held two forts that guarded the mouth of Mobile Bay. In 1864, the Union was anxious to seize the port of Mobile in order to strengthen its blockade of southern ports. Union naval officer David G. Farragut led a fleet of wooden frigates and four ironclad monitors to attack Mobile. His plan was to send the ironclads in first, followed by the wooden ships lashed together in pairs. Although one of the monitors was sunk by fire from the two Confederate forts, Farragut drove the rest of the fleet forward into the bay. He roared out an order that became legendary: "Damn the torpedoes! Full speed ahead!"

Though nearly ten times as many Union troops as Confederates were killed during the Battle of Mobile Bay, the Union forces achieved their goal of blockading the bay and port of Mobile. The city itself, however, held out against Union forces until 1865.

Chapter 6
AFTER THE WAR

AFTER THE WAR

Terrible inflation created great economic hardship throughout Alabama during the Civil War. Many historians agree, however, that the nine years of postwar Reconstruction were even more difficult for southerners.

RECONSTRUCTION

After the war, Alabama remained under military rule until 1868, when it was readmitted to the Union. For the next six years, the state was run by administrators from the North, called "carpetbaggers," and southerners who cooperated with them, called "scalawags." Whereas most white southerners were Democrats, the so-called scalawags were Republicans.

In 1867, the Ku Klux Klan, which had been founded in Tennessee, began to appear in northern Alabama. Klan members, who believed in white supremacy, gathered together to terrorize blacks and white Republicans in order to keep them from voting and exercising other rights. Riding at night on horseback and disguised behind white robes and hoods, they burned houses, captured blacks, and then whipped or even lynched (murdered) them.

The Democrats regained political control of the state in 1874, and the Reconstruction period came to an end. For many years to come, the Democratic party would dominate the state politically.

The Civil War took a heavy toll on Alabama's industry and agriculture. This 1865 engraving shows the ruins of a Confederate foundry in Selma.

THE POSTWAR ECONOMY

Alabama's economy was in disastrous shape after the war. Factories, mills, and ironworks had shut down. Railroads were worn out or had been partially destroyed. Farms had been overrun; livestock had been confiscated or stolen; there was no seed with which to plant new crops. Many banks had closed, and there was a severe money shortage. The inflation that had begun during the war became even worse. During the first postwar winter, many Alabamians nearly starved.

The position of freed slaves was especially unstable. Most of them were penniless and without any immediate means of making a living. Many remained in the shacks they had lived in on the plantations, working for their former masters for not much more than food and a leaky roof over their heads. Many others left the area to seek work elsewhere. In the Black Belt, Alabama's cotton country, black residents outnumbered whites, a situation that made many whites nervous. At the same time, planters were

This 1902 photograph shows a family of sharecroppers near Snow Hill, Alabama.

anxious to hang onto the cheap work force represented by former slaves and were worried that large numbers of blacks would move away.

The new relationship between blacks and whites led to a reorganization of the agricultural economy. Whites had no money to hire farmhands, and blacks were anxious to have more independence, so a tenant-farming or "sharecropping" system developed. Landowners provided the fields for growing crops, and sharecroppers provided the labor for a share of the crop.

The Fourteenth Amendment to the Constitution, which became law in 1868, was an attempt by Congress to prevent the states from discriminating against any citizen because of race. It stated that any state that interfered with the right to vote in federal elections could lose some of its representation in Congress. This law has never been enforced, however. For nearly a hundred years, the federal government simply ignored the fact that most southern states used a variety of methods, some of them violent, to keep blacks from voting or gaining significant political power.

EDUCATION

Educational opportunities were scarce for white children and almost nonexistent for blacks at the close of the Civil War. Gradually, a few schools were established.

A state public-school system had been established in 1854. In 1872, the State Agricultural and Mechanical College, which eventually became Auburn University, was established to provide industrial education for whites. The Talladega Institute for the Deaf, established in the 1850s, was enlarged after the war, and an institute for the blind was added. Agricultural schools were founded at Athens and Evergreen.

Julia Tutwiler, an Alabama woman who was determined to get an education at a time when this was a very unusual ambition for a well-bred southern woman, graduated from Vassar College. In 1882, she founded Livingston Normal School, now called Livingston University, for the training of women teachers. Her efforts also brought about the establishment of the Alabama Girls' Industrial School at Montevallo in 1895.

Even during the Reconstruction period, some white leaders saw the need for schools for blacks and worked with black leaders to establish them. A few planters had set up such schools in the hope that this would help to prevent their workers from migrating to other parts of the country. One of the first and most important schools established for young blacks was Tuskegee Normal and Industrial Institute.

Booker T. Washington, who founded Tuskegee Institute, believed that a practical education was the best way for American blacks to begin to make economic progress.

TUSKEGEE INSTITUTE

Booker T. Washington was a young man in his twenties when, in 1881, he was chosen to organize and head Tuskegee Institute. Washington had been born a slave, in Virginia, in 1856. Largely self-educated, he eventually attended Hampton Institute in Virginia, where he learned industrial skills. His natural teaching ability soon became apparent. He had been teaching at Hampton for two years when he was asked to come to Tuskegee to found a similar school.

Washington was wise and skillful in dealing with people. He willingly accepted advice and counsel from whites in order to advance the cause of his school and its students. He stated publicly that any progress in "the elevation of the Southern Negro must have to a certain extent the cooperation of Southern whites." He also convinced many conservative white leaders that an

A history class at Tuskegee Institute in 1902

educated black labor force would be an economic advantage to the South. Tuskegee offered blacks a practical, vocational education. The school was based on Washington's philosophy that acquiring practical job skills was the best way for blacks to make economic and social gains.

For more than a century, Tuskegee Institute has been a major force in improving conditions for blacks. Booker T. Washington firmly believed that education was the pathway out of poverty and weakness, and generations of students benefited from his vision and his administrative skills. Gradually, from the students at Tuskegee and a small handful of other black schools, a new black middle class developed — teachers, lawyers, doctors, skilled workers, and business leaders.

Even so, most southern blacks in the late 1800s remained very poor, and few had any power or influence outside their own communities.

GEORGE WASHINGTON CARVER

Over the years, many of the most important names in black American history were connected with Tuskegee Institute. George Washington Carver, who joined the faculty of the institute in 1896, gained widespread fame for his successful agricultural research-and-development programs. Born a slave, Carver had a boundless thirst for knowledge. He worked his way through high school, college, and graduate school, earning a master's degree in agriculture and learning everything he could about plant life. In his spare time, he studied music and art.

Carver was particularly interested in developing new and useful products from two plants grown in abundance by poor southern farmers—peanuts and sweet potatoes. He is credited with having developed some three hundred products from peanuts and one hundred from sweet potatoes. Even after he became internationally recognized and honored for his achievements, Dr. Carver remained a humble man, more interested in service than in fame or wealth.

INDUSTRY

When European settlers first arrived in Alabama, they referred to the Indians who were living in the mountains near present-day Birmingham as the "Red Sticks." This was because the Indians painted their faces and weapons with red "sticks" that were actually rocks rich in iron ore.

In the late 1800s, Birmingham became one of the nation's leading producers of iron and steel.

Alabama is rich in mineral resources, particularly coal and iron. The first iron furnace in the state was constructed in 1818. During the Civil War, sixteen Alabama ironworks produced nearly all the iron used by the Confederacy for shot, shells, and rifles. Munitions were fabricated at plants in Selma and Irondale.

After several difficult postwar years, economic recovery started gradually and continued through the 1870s and 1880s. The iron, and later steel, industry grew in importance in northern Alabama. By the 1890s, iron and steel making had become the most important industry in the state.

Land speculators gambled on the future of this mineral-rich part of the state and, in 1871, founded a town that they called Birmingham. One of the members of this group, John Milner, was chief engineer of a railroad. He correctly believed that two railroads would eventually cross at that location.

Tannehill Historical State Park near Bessemer preserves the ruins of
the Tannehill Ironworks.

Today, Birmingham is the state's largest city. Like the industrial
city in England for which it was named, Birmingham was
destined to be an important industrial center. It got off to a slow
and shaky start, however. A cholera epidemic, combined with a
nationwide economic panic, nearly wiped out the fledgling
settlement only two years after its founding.

A story is told about one man whose efforts helped keep
Birmingham alive. Charles Linn built a small bank in Birmingham
when the city was just getting started. In 1873, despite the twin
disasters of cholera and economic depression, he demonstrated his
faith in Birmingham's future by erecting a new, larger bank
building. Then, to celebrate its opening, he invited five hundred
guests to a dance. In recognition of the hard times, he called it a
Calico Ball. All the guests wore formal clothing made of calico.
Even the men's fashionable tuxedos were tailored out of the
inexpensive cotton material.

The Tannehill Ironworks in Bessemer, near Birmingham, had been a major supplier of cannonballs and gun parts for the Confederate forces during the war. In addition to vast supplies of iron, the area around Birmingham has plentiful deposits of coal and limestone, two other raw materials used in the production of steel. The city rapidly became a major producer of iron and steel products. It had both the necessary raw materials and a labor force of thousands of southerners who needed employment and were willing to work for relatively low wages. The nation had moved into an industrial period, and the demand for iron and steel was nearly unlimited.

Birmingham soon became known as the Pittsburgh of the South. Between 1880 and 1890, its population exploded from three thousand to twenty-six thousand people. More than twenty other ironmaking boomtowns, including Anniston, Gadsden, Bessemer, and Ensley, also sprang up during this time.

Other industries began developing in the state in the late 1880s—railroading, shipping, lumbering, textile manufacturing, and the manufacturing of products from cottonseed oil. Even so, at the turn of the century, 88 percent of Alabama's people still lived on farms.

In 1907, United States Steel, the nation's largest steel-making company, came to Alabama. For a number of years, most of the hard, backbreaking jobs in the mills were held by convicts. The state justified the system because it was cheaper to lease prisoners to the steel companies than to build expensive prisons. But the convicts were cruelly treated, and their cheap labor was robbing other citizens of jobs. Reformers succeeded in abolishing the practice in 1928. Child labor, too, was common until the mid-1930s. Children as young as six or seven were forced to work long hours for only a few pennies a day.

Chapter 7

THE TWENTIETH CENTURY

THE TWENTIETH CENTURY

As the twentieth century began, Alabama still had not completely recovered financially from the effects of the Civil War and the Reconstruction period. Both whites and blacks struggled to make ends meet.

A new state constitution adopted in 1901 was a giant step backward for race relations and democratic government in Alabama. Voting qualifications were made very difficult; a man had to prove that he was literate and employed or that he owned three hundred dollars' worth of taxable property. He also had to pay a poll tax. Final decisions about who met these requirements were made by a county's board of registrars. As a result, thousands of blacks and poor whites were disenfranchised. This deplorable situation was to continue for the next sixty years.

WORLD WAR I

More than eighty-six thousand men from Alabama joined the armed forces during World War I. The war was economically beneficial to Alabama, as Mobile's shipbuilding industry flourished and farmers stepped up production to meet the nation's wartime needs for food and cotton.

Alabama's system of waterways had always been one of its most important assets. The Tennessee River, a major river, cuts across the northern part of the state, flowing westward before it turns north to meet the Ohio River at Paducah, Kentucky. After the steamboat was invented in the early 1800s, people wanted to use this route for shipping and transportation. However, there was a major obstacle. At one point where the river became very shallow, a mass of jagged rocks made boat passage impossible. This 37-mile (60-kilometer) stretch was known as Muscle Shoals. Three times, companies were formed to build canals around the shoals, but none of the attempts was successful.

During the war, the nation needed manufacturing plants for the production of synthetic nitrate, a substance used in making munitions. President Woodrow Wilson selected Muscle Shoals as the site for two of these plants. His plan also called for a dam to be created on the Tennessee River. The dam would serve two functions. It would create a deep lake that would bury the shoals and make navigation possible, and the waterpower created by the dam could be used to make electricity to power the manufacturing plant.

The war ended almost as soon as the plants were built and before the dam was even completed. For several years, the federal government debated over how to use the facilities. The plants were put up for sale, and Henry Ford offered to buy them at a small fraction of their original cost, but the government declined to accept his offer. In 1924, the United States Army Corps of Engineers finished building Wilson Dam, the first of many dams to be built on the Tennessee River and its tributaries. Congress continued to debate about how to use the dam and the nitrate facility until 1933.

THE GREAT DEPRESSION AND THE NEW DEAL

The 1930s were years of widespread depression and unemployment throughout the United States. Alabama was

An Alabama farm family eating a dinner of biscuits and beans during the Great Depression of the 1930s

especially hard hit. It was still primarily an agricultural state, and two-thirds of its farmers were tenant farmers. The annual income of people in the Tennessee Valley was far below the national average. Many people could not read or write, and most had no specialized job skills.

About half of the approximately 3 million people who lived in the Tennessee Valley region were tenant farmers. Most of them grew corn, cotton, or tobacco. Soil erosion was a serious problem, and more and more farmland was abandoned as the soil became depleted. Forests were cut down without reforestation, and frequent forest fires destroyed additional wooded land. Most farmers lived in poorly built shacks that had no electricity. Malaria and health problems caused by poor nutrition were common.

Franklin Delano Roosevelt became president of the United States in 1933. Almost immediately, he introduced a recovery program that he called the New Deal, in which Congress would establish a number of federal agencies and programs to help farmers, laborers, and unemployed people.

Young men who joined the Civilian Conservation Corps (CCC) were given jobs improving state parks and planting trees to prevent soil erosion. The National Youth Administration (NYA) provided work for students, assisting them to continue their education in high schools and colleges. The Public Works Administration (PWA) put adults to work building structures for public use—post offices, libraries, dams, and bridges. The Works Progress Administration (WPA) provided other types of jobs.

Alabama farmers were helped by such New Deal measures as subsidies, soil-conservation programs, and agricultural education programs. Credit was made available so that farmers could buy land. The Rural Electrification Administration (REA) made inexpensive electricity available in rural areas. The New Deal raised wages, shortened the number of hours a person could be forced to work in a week, and ended child labor.

Labor unions were growing in many parts of the country at this time. The New Deal helped protect the rights of people who wanted to join unions. In Alabama, unions were successful in recruiting miners and steel workers, but most textile workers remained nonunion.

Several Alabamians were staunch supporters of Roosevelt and the New Deal. Senator Lister Hill worked hard to establish the Tennessee Valley Authority (TVA) and laws that benefited labor. Senators John Bankhead and Hugo Black and Speaker of the House William B. Bankhead were all prominent New Dealers. The New Deal appealed to Alabamians because it represented a kind of populist tradition—a concern for ordinary people and a suspicion of big corporations and Wall Street.

Such beautiful reservoirs as Guntersville Lake are among the benefits Alabamians have reaped from the TVA.

THE TENNESSEE VALLEY AUTHORITY

The year 1933 was marked by the establishment of the federal agency that was to have the greatest effect on the daily life of Alabama residents. On May 18, an act of Congress created the Tennessee Valley Authority (TVA), an agency charged with "planning for the proper use, conservation, and development of the natural resources of the Tennessee River drainage basin and its adjoining territory for the general social and economic welfare of the nation." The act outlined many goals for the TVA, including flood control, improvement of navigation, reforestation of the lands in the valley, agricultural and industrial development, and the operation of defense plants at Muscle Shoals.

By the late 1930s, five TVA hydroelectric facilities, powered by the water behind huge dams, were in operation. Three of these dams—Wilson, Wheeler, and Guntersville—were located in Alabama. Electricity was now available in areas where it had never been before, and at rates that ordinary people could afford.

The TVA set up a program to help people buy electrical appliances and teach them how to use them. For the first time, farmers could install refrigeration for their dairy products, pumps that brought running water into their homes, and electrically heated incubators for their chicks.

World War II dominated the thoughts of the American people during the early 1940s. The TVA rushed to complete more dams in order to provide hydroelectric power for new war plants built in the area. Alabama soon became one of the country's largest arsenals. After the war, many of these factories shifted to producing goods for peacetime use.

OTHER ACCOMPLISHMENTS OF THE TVA

In 1952, the navigation channel of the Tennessee River was completed. By 1959, 12 million tons (10.9 million metric tons) of freight were being carried through the channel. New industries attracted by the availability of low-cost power and easy transportation had sprung up all along the way.

Flood control, another major purpose of the TVA projects, was put to the test in 1957 when prolonged storms dumped record amounts of rain on the region. The agency estimated that more than $100 million in property damage was prevented by the TVA's flood-control systems.

Recreational facilities are another by-product of the TVA. In Alabama, as in the other seven states served by the agency, TVA dams have created large, beautiful lakes. These artificial lakes are used for swimming, boating, fishing, and other water sports, and the lands bordering them provide opportunities for camping and other outdoor activities.

The TVA has also initiated programs to help farmers make use of modern agricultural methods. Researchers at the National Fertilizer Development Center at Muscle Shoals work on finding ways to increase crop production.

WORLD WAR II

The 1940s had ushered in a few changes for blacks in the South. Shortly before World War II began, President Roosevelt instructed the army to begin a training program for black pilots. Tuskegee was chosen as the location of a pilot program. Some black leaders welcomed this facility and the new job opportunities it offered the black community. Others who wanted to see progress toward an integrated society were strongly opposed to the fact that the program was strictly segregated.

Huntsville, Alabama's northernmost major city, played a key role for the United States during World War II. In 1941, two months before the Japanese bombed Pearl Harbor, the city became the site of the Redstone Ordnance Plant, later renamed Redstone Arsenal. Its focus was the development and production of rockets and guided missiles, an area of weaponry in which the Germans were far ahead of the United States.

Although the United States and its allies defeated Germany, at the end of the war the United States was still behind Germany in rocket technology. In 1945, German scientist Dr. Wernher von Braun and most of his staff surrendered to American troops. He and 116 other German rocket experts arrived in the United States in September of that year to develop missiles for the United States government.

In 1950, von Braun and his team of scientists were transferred from Fort Bliss in Texas to Redstone Arsenal at Huntsville to

GEMINI
SPACE SUIT

EARTH'S LARGEST SPACE MUSEUM
HUNTSVILLE, ALABAMA

Redstone Arsenal in Huntsville, established in 1941, became an important rocket and spacecraft development center. In 1960, NASA opened the George C. Marshall Space Flight Center in Huntsville. Today, displays at the Alabama Space and Rocket Center celebrate the contributions Huntsville has made to American space technology.

develop guided missiles. In 1958, the first American satellite, powered by the Jupiter rocket developed by von Braun and his team, was launched into orbit. Later that year, the National Aeronautics and Space Administration (NASA) was established. In 1960, NASA established the new George C. Marshall Space Flight Center at Redstone Arsenal. Since then, Huntsville has proudly called itself "Rocket City, USA."

Over the years, von Braun and his team were responsible for developing other important missiles and rockets at Huntsville, including the Redstone Rocket that launched America's first astronaut into space, and the huge Saturn rockets used to launch the Apollo missions to the moon. In fact, every American voyage into space has been made possible through the use of rockets developed at Huntsville. As a result, Huntsville has been transformed from a small, sleepy, southern city into an international science center.

JIM CROW

Today, one might not recognize the way of life that all southern blacks endured in the 1940s. All public facilities were segregated. Restaurants, hotels, and theaters were for either whites or blacks; almost none of them—with a very few exceptions such as federal cafeterias—served both. Bus and railroad stations had separate waiting rooms and rest rooms. Even self-service coin laundries had machines labeled For Colored Only

Discrimination against blacks had a name in those days—Jim Crow. Signs that said For Whites Only were known as Jim Crow signs; state laws enforcing segregation were Jim Crow laws. For many black Americans, the experience of World War II brought about an increased desire to challenge Jim Crow. Many blacks who served in the armed forces came home after the war with a new outlook. As one veteran said, "After being overseas fighting for democracy, I thought that when we got back here we should enjoy a little of it."

A major wound was inflicted on Jim Crow in 1946, when the United States Supreme Court made it illegal to force black passengers to sit in the rear seats of buses and trains that crossed state lines. Although this was one step toward desegregation, it applied only to interstate transportation. City buses could still enforce the rule of whites in front, blacks in back.

A few years later, in 1954, another Supreme Court decision stated that compulsory segregation in public schools denies equal protection under the law as guaranteed by the Constitution. The next year, the court ordered that schools should be desegregated "with all deliberate speed."

These rulings had an immediate effect on all the states— including Alabama—that up until then had relied on state laws to keep segregation in force. Times were changing, slowly, and black leaders began looking for ways to speed up the changes.

Hundreds of schools were integrated over the next few years, and many civil-rights cases were tried in various state and federal courts. Courtrooms, however, were not the only places where the drama of change was being played out.

THE CIVIL RIGHTS MOVEMENT IN ALABAMA

Alabama soon found itself to be the center stage of the Civil Rights Movement. On a December afternoon in 1955, a black woman boarded a city bus in Montgomery. Worn out from working all day as a seamstress, Mrs. Rosa Parks sank into the nearest empty seat. When ordered to give up her seat to a white passenger, she refused—and was arrested.

Mrs. Parks had no idea that this small, rebellious act would put her name in the history books. She was not planning to start a nationwide movement, but she was aware of recent Supreme Court decisions, and believed she had as much right to a seat on a bus as anyone else.

News of what had happened spread through Montgomery's black community like wildfire. Dr. Martin Luther King, Jr., the new pastor of a local black Baptist church, urged his congregation and others in the city to protest Mrs. Parks' arrest and the segregation policy of the city bus system. King strongly believed that peaceful demonstrations were the best way to bring about social change. His philosophy of nonviolent protest was borrowed from the work of Mahatma Gandhi, the great leader who helped India gain its independence from the British Empire. Believing that a boycott would be an effective weapon, he urged all of Montgomery's black citizens to stay off the city buses.

For months, Montgomery's blacks refused to ride the buses, instead choosing to walk, form car pools, or stay home. The boycott was even observed by many who lived miles from their jobs. As the boycott went on, downtown businesses began to feel its effects. Finally, after more than a year, the United States Supreme Court ruled that bus segregation was unconstitutional. The victory was a morale booster for everyone who hoped that equality could be brought about by peaceful means.

By the early 1960s, it was obvious that the Civil Rights Movement was not something that was going to disappear. Discrimination in jobs, housing, education, and public facilities was not limited to the South, and peaceful "sit-ins" were held at many locations in both the North and the South during the early 1960s.

Despite the 1954 Supreme Court decision calling for integration of public schools, few blacks had yet been admitted to southern state universities. In the spring of 1963, a federal judge ordered the enrollment of two black students at the University of Alabama. Governor George C. Wallace, knowing that most of his constituents were opposed to integration, had made a campaign

In the 1950s and 1960s, Reverend Martin Luther King, Jr. (left), pastor at Montgomery's Dexter Avenue Baptist Church (above), led a number of peaceful demonstrations and marches in Alabama to end racial segregation and discrimination in America.

pledge to stand in the doorway of the school, if necessary, to block the students' entrance. Wallace carried out this symbolic gesture because he wanted to demonstrate that he would give in only when forced to do so by the federal government. Assistant Attorney General Nicholas Katzenbach brought a unit of the Alabama National Guard to the university and confronted the governor. After making a short public statement, the governor stepped aside, and the two black students entered the building and registered.

Other events of 1963 were not as peaceful. Mass demonstrations in Birmingham were met with cruel force by the police. A bomb was thrown into the Sixteenth Avenue Baptist Church in Birmingham, killing four young black girls who had arrived to attend Sunday school.

Congress passed a Civil Rights Act in 1964 that forbade discrimination on the basis of a person's color, race, national origin, religion, or sex. The act guaranteed every American's right

Fire hoses were
used to break
up civil-rights
demonstrations
in Birmingham
in 1963.

to use public facilities, vote, and seek employment; and banned
discrimination by any programs receiving federal aid. But even
though the act overruled state laws that had upheld segregation,
enforcement of the new federal law did not immediately follow its
passage.

THE SELMA MARCHES

Late in 1964, Dr. King and the staff of the Southern Christian
Leadership Conference, an organization he headed, decided that
the time had come to wage a massive campaign to secure voting
rights for Alabama's blacks. The city of Selma, seat of Dallas
County, was chosen as the site of the protest. Only about 350 of
the county's 15,000 eligible blacks had managed to register to vote.

The Civil Rights Act of 1964 had called for integration of public
accommodations. However, when Dr. King and his party came to
Selma in January of 1965 at the invitation of local blacks, no
integration had yet occurred. King made a public announcement

On March 10, 1965, demonstrators intending to march from Selma to Montgomery to campaign for black voting rights were turned back by state troopers. Later that month, however, Martin Luther King, Jr., led a successful march from Selma to Montgomery. This massive protest led to passage of the Voting Rights Act of 1965.

that he would test enforcement of the law by registering at a fine, old, local hotel. The hotel management and city restaurant owners decided not to defy the law, so Dr. King was given a room, and Selma's public accommodations were integrated peacefully.

Securing voting rights, however, was another matter. February and March were months of turmoil. Hundreds of blacks who tried to register in Selma were prevented from doing so. Protest marches were held day after day. Many marchers were arrested; some were treated roughly by local police. After a few weeks, Dr. King announced that demonstrators would carry out a protest march from Selma to the state capitol in Montgomery. By early March, local black marchers had been joined by whites—some of them concerned Alabama citizens, others from many other parts of the country. In all, more than twenty-five thousand people participated in the massive protest.

On March 15, President Lyndon Johnson made a stirring speech to the nation, stating that Congress had the constitutional responsibility to assure all citizens the right to vote. When a demonstrator from Detroit named Mrs. Viola Liuzzo was ambushed and shot in her car near Montgomery by four Ku Klux Klansmen, President Johnson again appeared on television. He announced that the murderers had been arrested, and declared that Klan members were "enemies of justice who for decades have used the rope and the gun and tar and feathers" to terrorize blacks.

The completion of the march was a triumph for thousands of black Alabamians who long had lived with little hope of taking part in democracy, or even of living without fear of local terrorism.

THE CIVIL RIGHTS MOVEMENT WAS A START

In his 1949 Christmas message to the state, Alabama governor James Folsom said, "As long as the Negroes are held down by deprivation and lack of opportunity, all the other people will be held down alongside them. Let's start talking fellowship and brotherly love, and doing unto others. And let's do more than talk about it; let's start living it."

Some of the most tragic and dramatic events of the Civil Rights Movement of the 1960s took place in Alabama. Since then, significant strides toward better race relations have been made, although there is still room for improvement. Poverty and unemployment in counties with a predominantly black population are still much higher than in other parts of the state. Efforts to bring new industry into these counties have not been very successful.

Still, progress has been made. Alabamians can, and do, point with pride to many changes that have been made since the stormy sixties. The Selma demonstrations and the march from Selma to

In 1966, as a result of the Voting Rights Act, thousands of black Alabamians registered to vote for the first time.

Montgomery led directly to the passage of the Voting Rights Act of 1965. In this act, Congress banned educational tests and other discriminatory procedures that had been used as a means of depriving blacks of the right to vote. Five times as many Alabama blacks were registered to vote in 1984 as in 1960. Public schools have been desegregated, and new, integrated, technical and junior colleges have been built.

Advocates of white supremacy still commit occasional acts of terrorism, but such acts are usually quickly punished rather than ignored as they once were. Governor Wallace, who in his 1963 inaugural address promised, "Segregation now! Segregation tomorrow! Segregation forever!" eventually changed his views. During his four separate terms as governor, he appointed many blacks to state offices.

Today, official city and state publications proclaim proudly not only that Montgomery is the Cradle of the Confederacy—but also that it was the birthplace of the Civil Rights Movement.

Chapter 8
GOVERNMENT AND THE ECONOMY

GOVERNMENT AND THE ECONOMY

Alabama's present constitution was adopted in 1901. It is the longest state constitution in the United States, and has been amended more than 440 times.

STATE GOVERNMENT

As in most other states, Alabama's government is divided into three branches—executive, judicial, and legislative. The legislature consists of two houses: a senate with 35 members, and a house of representatives with 105 members. All members of the legislature are elected to four-year terms.

Elected members of the executive branch include the governor, lieutenant governor, secretary of state, attorney general, treasurer, auditor, and members of the board of education and the public service commission. The governor is elected to a four-year term and cannot serve more than two terms in succession. He or she must be at least thirty years old, a United States citizen for ten years, and a citizen of Alabama for seven years.

The Alabama supreme court, the state's highest court, has nine members, all of whom are elected to six-year terms. The court of criminal appeals has five judges and the civil-appeals court has three judges. Alabama has several lower courts, including circuit, district, probate, and municipal courts.

POLITICAL PARTIES

For many years following the Civil War, Alabama was a part of the Solid South—meaning that the majority of its people could be counted on to vote for the Democratic party. For the most part, when voting in state elections, both black and white voters in Alabama remain loyal to the Democratic party. In national elections, however, these loyalties have been seriously strained for the last four decades. The Democratic party has carried Alabama in only four of the last ten presidential elections.

In 1948, many southern Democrats bolted from the Democratic party because they objected to its position on civil rights. These southerners formed a third party called the States' Rights Democratic party, nicknamed the Dixiecrats. Their candidate for president was South Carolina governor J. Strom Thurmond. Alabama was one of four southern states whose electoral votes went to Thurmond.

A majority of the state's voters returned to the Democratic party for the next three presidential elections, but in 1964, Republican candidate Barry Goldwater carried the state. Alabama governor George Wallace led another third party, the American Independent party, in 1968. He carried his state and four others that year. Since then, the state's electoral votes have gone to Republican Richard Nixon in 1972, Democrat Jimmy Carter in 1976, and Republican Ronald Reagan in 1980 and 1984.

EDUCATION

Because Alabama has struggled economically through much of its history, it has not been able to spend as much on public education as have many other states. According to the 1980

The University of Alabama at Birmingham

census, one-fourth of the adult population had attended eight years of school or less. Only a little more than half of the adults in Alabama had graduated from high school.

Despite the efforts of the federal government to end segregation in public schools, in 1980 one-fourth of all minority pupils in Alabama were attending schools that were 99 to 100 percent minority. Many white families send their children to segregated private schools, especially in the counties where a majority of the residents are black. The cost of maintaining two separate school systems—one public and one private—is great, and the quality of both systems suffers.

There are sixty institutions of higher learning in the state. Of these, twenty-one are public two-year colleges, sixteen are public four-year institutions, and twenty-three are private colleges. The major state universities are the University of Alabama, with campuses at Tuscaloosa, Birmingham, and Huntsville; and Auburn University.

Textiles (above) and twine (right) are among
the many products manufactured in Alabama.

THE ECONOMY

The Industrial Revolution came to Alabama in the 1870s, when
the state's coal, iron, and steel industries began booming. Since the
mid-1970s, heavy manufacturing has been decreasing in
importance compared to other segments of the state's economy.
Even so, manufacturing is still Alabama's single most-important
economic activity. Alabama's major manufactured products are
clothing and other textiles, paper and allied products, rubber and
plastics products, primary metals, food products, and chemicals
and allied products.

When compared with the other forty-nine states, Alabama
ranks close to the middle on quite a few counts. It is twenty-ninth
in size, twenty-second in population, twenty-sixth in retail trade,
twenty-sixth in agricultural income, and twenty-second in
mineral production.

However, the residents of forty-three other states are better off
financially, on the average, than Alabamians. The average per
capita (individual) income in Alabama is only about 80 percent of
the national average, and one of every seven people in the state is
living below what the government defines as the poverty level. In

general, the greatest poverty is found in the Black Belt. In the mid-1980s, the unemployment rate of Alabama was higher than that of all except two other states, and it was more than twice as high for blacks as for whites.

THE FARMS

Cotton became the main agricultural crop in Alabama by the middle of the nineteenth century. So much land was planted with cotton that some other necessary products, such as corn, had to be brought in from outside the state. By 1880, every county in Alabama was producing at least some cotton.

Eventually, farmers realized that when only one crop is grown on the same soil year after year, certain nutrients needed by that crop are used up and the land becomes "worn out." The way to avoid this is to rotate crops—plant different crops in different years and give the soil a chance to renew itself. By the early 1900s, large tracts of Alabama farmland had become badly worn by one-crop farming. At the same time, an insect called the Mexican boll weevil began destroying Alabama's cotton crop. As a result, many Alabama farmers began to switch from cotton to livestock or other crops. This turned the economy around, and before long, people recognized that the boll weevil had been a blessing in disguise. In the town of Enterprise, there is a monument to the boll weevil— probably the only monument in the world that pays tribute to a pest. Between 1930 and 1980, cotton acreage decreased by 90 percent, from 3.5 million acres (1.4 million hectares) to 350,000 acres (141,640 hectares).

Today, soybeans, peanuts, corn, wheat, vegetables (principally tomatoes and sweet potatoes), and pecans are Alabama's major crops. Livestock and dairy products are also important, especially

The port facilities at Mobile, Alabama's only seaport, are considered among the finest in the United States.

the Panama Canal. The port city of Mobile benefits greatly from the project, because it is now connected to a network of major waterways that serves most of the eastern United States. Hundreds of millions of dollars' worth of cargo passes through Mobile, Alabama's only international port, each year.

A state highway department was established in 1911. Before then, roads in Alabama had been built by private companies. Today, Alabama has about 97,000 miles (156,106 kilometers) of roads and highways and about 4,500 miles (7,242 kilometers) of railroad track. The state is served by about 145 airports, the busiest of which is in Birmingham.

Alabama has about 240 radio stations and 25 television stations. The State Educational Television Commission operates 9 of the stations.

The oldest newspaper in the state is the *Mobile Register,* founded in 1813. Alabama has about 100 newspapers, about 30 of which are dailies. The *Birmingham News* is the giant among them; its circulation is more than three times as high as any other Alabama city paper. *Southern Living* is a highly successful regional magazine based in Birmingham.

Chapter 9

ARTS AND RECREATION

ARTS AND RECREATION

Alabama has a rich heritage of traditional, or folk, arts. Traditional arts are those that have been passed from one generation to the next by members of a family or community.

TRADITIONAL AMERICAN FOLK ART

Pioneer America had no shopping malls, supermarkets, or mail-order catalogues. Consequently, people had to make all kinds of everyday items for themselves, including clothes, dishes, toys, and furniture. Naturally, some of the artisans turned out items of high artistic quality. But because these crafts have such humble and functional origins, they have often been ignored or overlooked as art objects. When the nation turned its attention to a celebration of its bicentennial in the 1970s, many people "discovered" traditional American arts. Interest in quilting, pottery making, and similar arts was revived.

THE ALABAMA ARTS COUNCIL

The Alabama Arts Council is an organization that gives grants, received from the National Endowment for the Arts and the Alabama state legislature, to encourage a variety of artistic efforts. Recognizing the importance of preserving Alabama's traditional art heritage, the council has created the Alabama Folk Life

Two crafts that are part of Alabama's rich folk heritage are quilt making (left) and candle making (right).

Program, which pays artists to use some of their time to teach their skills to young apprentices.

For example, one grant was given to an artisan whose family had been making pottery in northern Alabama for nine generations. Another went to some Creek Indian women who are teaching others how to make baskets from white oak splints and pine straw. The Creeks have been making these baskets in the area since before the arrival of white settlers.

The purpose of the folk arts program is to help preserve traditional arts. The arts and crafts fairs that are held throughout Alabama each summer achieve the same purpose, and give artists a market for their products and programs.

TRADITIONAL MUSIC

Alabama is nationally recognized as an important center of traditional American music. Alabamians perform in concerts of

Alabama is recognized as an important center of traditional American music.

Negro spirituals, a cappella (without instrumental accompaniment) gospel songs, fiddle music, and Appalachian string-band music.

A string band consists primarily of banjos, fiddles, and guitars. The banjo is thought to be an Americanized African instrument, introduced to the United States by slaves. There are many string-band musicians in northern Alabama, and a few artisans in the region know how to make handcrafted banjos, mandolins, and fiddles.

Alabama has produced many musicians who have achieved national recognition for their work in many different types of popular music—jazz, blues, gospel, country, and rock. The strong musical tradition of northern Alabama's Tennessee Valley has also spawned a thriving recording industry. Several studios in the vicinity of Muscle Shoals are internationally known for the high quality of the recordings they produce.

One very popular country-music group is the band Alabama, which tours year-round but is based in Fort Payne. Every year,

In Birmingham, classical-music lovers enjoy the Alabama Symphony Orchestra (above) and the Birmingham Opera Theater (right).

the band hosts an open-air festival there, called "June Jam," that attracts big-name artists. The money generated by the festival is donated to local projects.

CLASSICAL PERFORMING ARTS

The Alabama Symphony Orchestra is the state's only professional symphony orchestra. Based in Birmingham, it performs during a forty-week concert season. Its Youth Concerts are presented to more than thirty-five thousand local school children and an estimated eighty thousand children in other parts of the state. Huntsville and Montgomery have symphony orchestras made up of volunteers; both are rapidly developing into regional orchestras.

Birmingham's Civic Opera (a performing company) and the Southern Regional Opera (a booking organization that brings opera performances in from outside the city) have recently merged and are now called the Birmingham Opera Theater.

A professional dance company, the State of Alabama Ballet, has grown out of a company that started on the campus of the University of Alabama at Birmingham. Principals of the company have gone on to perform with the American Ballet Theater, the New York City Ballet, the Atlanta Ballet, and other major dance companies.

Theater in Alabama includes the Birmingham Children's Theater, a repertory company in Huntsville, and community theaters in Mobile and Montgomery. But the queen of Alabama's theaters—and one of North America's major theater companies—is the Alabama Shakespeare Festival. The company was started in Anniston, Alabama, in 1972. Eventually, Montgomery businessman Winton M. Blount and his wife Carolyn persuaded the company to move to the capital city. The Blounts donated $21.5 million to build an elaborate performing-arts complex in Montgomery. The Alabama Shakespeare Festival includes two auditoriums, rehearsal halls, offices, and a snack bar and gift shop. A 200-acre (81-hectare) English-style park surrounds the building. The theater's season runs for about nine months; musical and dance programs are offered year-round.

The state of Alabama offers an enviable program for aspiring young artists. The Alabama School of Fine Arts, in Birmingham, is a state-supported boarding school. Students are admitted on the basis of auditions and pay no tuition. The curriculum includes dance, music, visual arts, theater, and creative writing.

MUSEUMS

Alabama has about sixty museums. The state's most important art museum is the Birmingham Museum of Art. A new facility for the Montgomery Museum of Fine Arts, adjacent to the Alabama

Clockwise from top left: The Birmingham Children's Theater; scene from an Alabama Shakespeare Festival production of *As You Like It*; the Birmingham Museum of Art; the restored Alabama Theater in Birmingham

Shakespeare Festival, opened in 1988. Winton Blount, who built the theater facility, has added an outstanding collection of American art to the new museum.

The Alabama Space and Rocket Center, in Huntsville, is the

Many Alabama football fans cheer for the University of Alabama's Crimson Tide.

National Aeronautic and Space Administration's largest facility and Alabama's most popular tourist attraction. Other outstanding museums in Alabama include the George Washington Carver Museum at Tuskegee University, the Women's Army Corps Museum at Fort McClellan, the United States Army Aviation Museum at Fort Rucker, the Motor Sports Hall of Fame Museum in Talladega, and the Museum of the City of Mobile.

SPORTS AND RECREATION

Collegiate football is not merely a spectator sport in Alabama — it's a fever. Football fans are fiercely proud of their University of Alabama team, the Crimson Tide. Nearly every year, the Crimson Tide is named among the top ten college teams in the nation. Since 1926, it has won three Rose Bowls, six Sugar Bowls, four Orange Bowls, and two Cotton Bowls. Auburn University, a traditional rival, won the Sugar Bowl contest in 1984 and tied in 1988.

The Heisman Trophy, the prestigious award given each year to the college football player who is considered the best in the nation, was named for John Heisman, coach at Auburn University

Alabama's lakes, rivers, and seacoast provide opportunities for swimming, fishing, canoeing (above), and sailing (right).

from 1895 to 1899. Ironically, it was not won by an Auburn player until 1971, when it went to Pat Sullivan.

In 1985, Auburn student Bo Jackson was awarded the Heisman Trophy. An all-round athlete, he earned letters in three sports as a freshman. Jackson became the number-one draft pick of the National Football League in 1986, but he decided to play professional baseball instead and joined the Kansas City Royals that same year.

Although Alabama is not represented by teams in any of the major sports leagues, Birmingham has a minor-league baseball club. Two professional stock-car races are held each year in Talladega: the Winston 500 in May and the Talladega 500 in July. Boat races are held every summer at Lake Eufaula and at Guntersville.

For lovers of the outdoors, Alabama is an area made to order. Facilities for camping, hiking, water sports, hunting, and fishing are available throughout the state. Besides many rivers and large lakes, the state has more than thirty-five thousand small ponds and lakes for freshwater fishing. Alabama's coastline is crowded with hundreds of commercial and private fishing boats.

Chapter 10

HIGHLIGHTS OF THE HEART OF DIXIE

HIGHLIGHTS OF THE HEART OF DIXIE

NORTHERN ALABAMA: MOUNTAINS AND LAKES

Mountains, lakes, rivers, and forests make northern Alabama a scenic delight. Campers, hikers, and other lovers of the outdoors can find thousands of acres in which to explore back roads and unspoiled scenery.

Early in the spring, when the redbud, dogwood, and plum trees burst into bloom, the colors of the woods change from gray and black to pink, white, and green. Wild orchids, azaleas, roses, geraniums, and Johnny-jump-ups carpet the ground. Lilies, Queen Anne's lace, and wild hydrangeas follow in summer. Waterfalls tumble down the hillsides, and cold streams rush through gorges and canyons.

Five huge man-made lakes—Wilson, Wheeler, Guntersville, Weiss, and Lewis Smith—have made this part of the state popular with boaters, fishermen, waterskiers, and swimmers. Several national fishing tournaments are held on these lakes each year. The huge locks and dams that created the lakes are impressive feats of engineering.

Wheeler Lake is also the site of Wheeler National Wildlife Refuge, where hundreds of thousands of migratory birds make their winter home. The bird community includes two dozen species of ducks, as well as Canada, snow, and blue geese. White-tailed deer, muskrat, beaver, bobcat, fox, raccoon, and opossum live in the woods surrounding the lake.

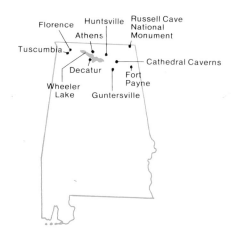

The Tennessee River near Stevenson in northeastern Alabama

The Givens Wildlife Interpretive Center is the South's largest educational center for the study of waterfowl and animals. The refuge is open to visitors year-round. In the winter, people can watch the birds through one-way glass windows in a heated observation building.

In Florence is the log-cabin birthplace of W.C. Handy, the jazz composer known as the "father of the blues." The home is now a museum, and Handy's piano, trumpet, and manuscripts are on display. Every August, jazz lovers congregate in Florence to listen to the music of some of the nation's best-known performers at the W.C. Handy Festival.

A few miles south of Florence, in Tuscumbia, is Ivy Green, the birthplace and childhood home of Helen Keller. An illness left Miss Keller both deaf and blind at the age of nineteen months. Yet, helped by her brilliant and determined teacher, Anne Sullivan, she learned to communicate through sign language, and eventually learned to speak. Keller graduated with honors from Radcliffe College and became an internationally known lecturer

Hot-air balloon races are held in Decatur during the city's annual Alabama Jubilee.

and writer. She spent much of her life traveling throughout the world to arouse interest in improving conditions for the disabled. Every June, a special festival is held in Tuscumbia to commemorate Helen Keller's remarkable life and achievements. *The Miracle Worker,* an award-winning play about her relationship with Anne Sullivan, is performed on Fridays and Saturdays for six weeks each summer.

At the end of the first week of October, traditional American music fills the air at the Tennessee Valley Old Time Fiddlers' Convention in Athens. The climax of the festival is the naming of the Tennessee Valley Fiddle King.

Point Mallard Park, in Decatur, is a recreational park on the Tennessee River that hosts several popular annual events. Alabama Jubilee, on Memorial Day weekend, features a series of hot-air balloon races. A huge Fourth of July celebration called the Spirit of America Festival is also held at the park. In November, the Southern Wildfowl Festival includes a duck-calling contest, as well as exhibitions of decoy carvings, artwork, and photography related to wildfowl.

Caves lie beneath some of the land in the northeast corner of

94

Cathedral Caverns (above) and Little River Canyon (right) are among the scenic wonders of northern Alabama.

the state. Russell Cave National Monument is considered to be one of the most important archaeological sites discovered in recent times. Many artifacts left behind by several different groups of prehistoric peoples have been found here. A huge, 20,000-square-foot (1,858-square-meter) cave is a part of a much larger, 1-mile- (1.6-kilometer-) long cavern. A visitor center with displays that tell about the life of the cave's former inhabitants is open all year, and a number of nature trails surround the center.

Cathedral Caverns, near Grant, have some of the world's largest stalagmites, towering 60 feet (18 meters) high and stretching 200 feet (61 meters) in circumference. Bluegrass festivals are held in the underground caverns.

South of Russell Cave, near the town of Fort Payne, are the Sequoyah Caverns. Here one can find spectacular rock formations, ancient fossils, mirrorlike underground lakes, and waterfalls. Dramatic lighting has been installed to create special effects. Little River Canyon, east of town, is the deepest canyon east of the

Mississippi River. Fort Payne is also the home of the annual June Jam, a major country-music festival produced by the band Alabama.

HUNTSVILLE AND GUNTERSVILLE

Huntsville is the "least southern city in the state" according to many residents of other Alabama cities. The fact that it is located farther north than any of the state's other population centers is not the only reason for its relative "un-southernness."

The presence of NASA's Marshall Space Flight Center has brought scientists and executives from all over the world to work either for the government or for the dozens of "high-tech" companies that have located here in the past few decades. These newcomers have brought new tastes, cultures, and ideas that fill the atmosphere of the city with energy and excitement. Although Huntsville has many preserved nineteenth-century homes and buildings, the central part of the city is sleek and modern and suggests the future more than it recalls the past.

First settled in 1805, Huntsville was primarily an agricultural center in its early days. Soon, land was cleared for huge cotton plantations, and a cotton-spinning factory began operating in 1818. By the end of the century, Huntsville was a thriving textile center. Cotton and other agricultural products are still grown in the area surrounding the city, but farming has been replaced in importance by industry—especially the aerospace industry—in the late twentieth century.

The Alabama Space and Rocket Center, which includes the world's largest space museum, is Alabama's most-visited tourist attraction. Visitors to the center can pilot a simulated spacecraft to the surface of the moon, fire laser beams, and feel the force of

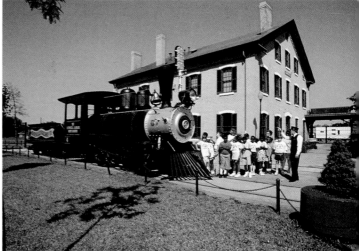

Huntsville's attractions include the Alabama Space and Rocket Center (left) and the Huntsville Depot (above).

triple gravity and zero gravity. One can see sixty different exhibits, get close enough to touch some of the rockets that actually went into space, and visit the center where rockets were developed and astronauts received part of their training.

Big Spring International Park, in the heart of the city, is filled with gifts donated by foreign countries, such as a sundial from the Federal Republic of Germany, cherry trees from Japan, a light beacon and tower from Norway, and a garden planted with roses sent from Switzerland. The Huntsville Depot, a restored 1860 railroad station, is an elaborate structure that illustrates the importance of railroad transportation to the city's development.

A number of people who work in Huntsville live in Guntersville, where they can enjoy all the recreational activities available on Guntersville Lake. Guntersville was a Cherokee village when early explorers came into the area in 1790. Andrew

Big Spring International Park in Huntsville is filled with gifts from foreign countries, such as these cherry trees from Japan.

Jackson camped near here during the Creek Indian War. He and Davy Crockett recruited a company of Cherokees to help them fight the Creeks. Much of the town was destroyed during the Civil War.

In 1939, Guntersville Dam was built. With new sources of power available, the city soon became an industrial center, and its population grew rapidly. Today it is an important river port for the shipping of such agricultural products as poultry, hogs, corn, soybeans, cattle, and pimientos.

BIRMINGHAM

Birmingham, the state's largest city, is also its newest, founded in 1871. The city grew up around a booming iron and steel industry. Today, however, the city's largest employer is the University of Alabama at Birmingham.

Two reminders of Birmingham's origin as an iron and steel center are the huge iron statue of Vulcan that overlooks the city from the top of Red Mountain (right), and the historic Sloss Furnaces (above).

Between 1881 and 1971, millions of tons of pig iron were processed at the Sloss Furnaces in Birmingham. The site has been designated a National Historic Landmark, and now includes a museum of industrial history and an auditorium that hosts symphony, jazz, and other types of musical concerts.

A giant statue of Vulcan, the Roman god of fire and metalworking, stands guard over Birmingham from the top of Red Mountain. The largest cast-iron statue in the world, the figure was designed as a symbol of the area's industry for an exhibit at the Louisiana Purchase Exposition in St. Louis in 1904.

In nearby Bessemer, Tannehill Historical State Park commemorates the birth of the region's iron and steel industry. The Tannehill Ironworks turned out cannonballs and gun barrels for the Confederate army until the complex was destroyed by the Eighth Iowa Cavalry. The park includes a restored furnace, pioneer houses, a gristmill, a cotton gin, and a country church.

CENTRAL ALABAMA: PLANTATION COUNTRY

Central Alabama is the true heart of the "Land of Cotton." Among the beautiful antebellum homes that are still standing and open to the public are Gaineswood in Demopolis, Sturdivant Hall in Selma, and Magnolia Grove in Greensboro. Spring pilgrimages to historic homes are held annually in such communities as Lowndesboro, Eufaula, Tuskegee, Selma, and Talladega.

Moundville is named for the mounds found in the area that were built for ceremonial purposes by prehistoric Indians. Mound State Monument includes the mounds, a reconstructed Indian village, burial grounds, and a museum.

Tuskegee is known around the world as the home of Tuskegee University, once called Tuskegee Institute. Tuskegee Institute National Historic Site was established by Congress in 1974. It includes The Oaks, Booker T. Washington's home; the Carver Museum, which has exhibits illustrating the important scientific work of George Washington Carver; and a visitor information center housed in Grey Columns, a two-story Greek Revival home built by slave labor. North of Tuskegee is Horseshoe Bend National Military Park, site of the final battle of the Creek War of 1813-14.

MONTGOMERY

Montgomery, Alabama's capital city, boasts of being the birthplace of three important milestones in American history: the Confederacy, in 1861; the country's first trolley system, in 1886; and the Civil Rights Movement, in 1955.

The Confederate States of America was established here at a convention of six seceding states in February 1861, and the first

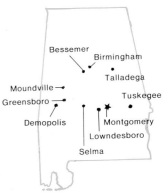

Magnolia Grove in Greensboro is one of many beautiful antebellum homes in central Alabama.

capital of the new nation was located in Montgomery. Several other cities dispute Montgomery's claim about the trolley cars, but Montgomery historians document the fact that this was the first city in the Western Hemisphere to have a city-wide electric trolley system. It operated from March 1886 until trolleys were replaced by buses in 1936. And when Montgomery citizen Rosa Parks defied the segregation laws that required blacks to yield their seats to whites, Montgomery became the site of the beginning of the Civil Rights Movement.

The First White House of the Confederacy, an 1835 Italianate-style structure, was the home of President and Mrs. Jefferson Davis. Open to the public as a house museum, it contains many of the Davis family's original furnishings and possessions.

An early period of local history is brought to life at the Old North Hull Street Historic District, which features a number of restored nineteenth-century buildings. A local writer has recorded a delightful guided tour that visitors can listen to as they look at the buildings.

The Dexter Avenue King Memorial Baptist Church in Montgomery played an important role in the Civil Rights

Movement. It was while Dr. Martin Luther King, Jr., was pastor at the church that he led the boycott of Montgomery's bus system, in 1955. The church is a red brick building that was completed in 1889. A historic mural on a wall in the basement depicts the major events of the movement and of Dr. King's life. Portraits of more than a dozen black leaders are included in the mural. The church has been named a National Historic Landmark.

Jasmine Hill Gardens, a landscaped sculpture garden, is one of Montgomery's most beautiful attractions. Concerts and festivals are held in its amphitheater. The newest pride and joy of Montgomery is the beautiful, lavish Winton M. Blount Cultural Park, home of the noted Alabama Shakespeare Festival and the Montgomery Museum of Fine Arts.

SOUTHERN ALABAMA

Southeastern Alabama is known as the Wiregrass area because of the tough grasses that had to be cleared before farmers could plant in the region. It is now an important agricultural area where soybeans, corn, and peanuts are grown.

At one time, cotton was the major crop of the region. But after 1910, the boll weevil began destroying so much of the crop every year that farmers were forced to begin diversifying. Later on, farmers recognized that the pest had actually done more good than harm for the area. A monument erected in the town of Enterprise reads, "In profound appreciation of the boll weevil and what it has done as the herald of prosperity."

Lake Eufaula, on the Georgia state line, is a favorite spot for bass fishing. Eufaula National Wildlife Refuge has an observation tower and a photography blind where people can watch geese, ducks, egrets, herons, and various kinds of small animals.

The port city of Mobile
lies on Mobile Bay at
Alabama's southeastern tip.

The southwestern corner of Alabama is largely a delta where some of the state's rivers empty into the Gulf of Mexico.

MOBILE

Mobile, the state's second-largest city, sits on the edge of Mobile Bay. Its prosperity has stemmed largely from its fine deep-water port. The port originally handled cotton shipped down the Tombigbee River by steamboat, then later handled iron and steel shipped from Birmingham. The Port of Mobile can accommodate thirty-three oceangoing vessels at one time. It has more than 50 acres (20 hectares) of warehouse space, and its elevators can hold 3 million bushels of grain. The first Confederate submarine, the *Huntley*, was built in Mobile during the Civil War. The city was a shipbuilding center during both World War I and World War II.

Many of Mobile's traditions and customs date from its French and Spanish beginnings. While other parts of the state were being settled by pioneers—mostly Anglo-Saxon—who came over the mountains from the eastern and northern states, Mobile was being passed back and forth between France and Spain. Mardi Gras, an annual tradition carried out in many American communities with a French-Catholic heritage, is celebrated enthusiastically in Mobile. In fact, Mobile claims to be the birthplace of Mardi Gras observances in the United States. The Mardi Gras carnival, a week-long celebration that ends on Shrove Tuesday, occurs in preparation for the fasting and sacrifice of Lent. Although historians disagree as to when Mardi Gras was first introduced into this country by French colonists, people from Mobile say it was started in 1703 or 1704 by Jean Baptiste Le Moyne, Sieur de Bienville. Mobile residents claim to have been observing Mardi Gras with parades and parties for a hundred years before it became a tradition in New Orleans. The festival was forgotten in Mobile during the dark days of the Civil War, but in 1866 or 1867 a man named Joseph Stillwell Cain revived the tradition as a way of raising the morale of Mobile residents. The Sunday before Mardi Gras is now called Joe Cain Day, a time for "raisin' Cain."

In the spring, the entire city of Mobile—and in fact much of southern Alabama—seems on fire with the brilliant shades of pink, coral, red, and purple azaleas. The streets are marked with a pink line designating the Azalea Trail, leading past 37 miles (60 kilometers) of private yards and public parks filled with showy plantings. Even the azaleas are related to the city's French heritage; the first plants were brought to Mobile from France in 1760.

Many special events are scheduled for the azalea-blooming season, so that everyone can enjoy the city when it is dressed in its most colorful finery. Fifty young women act as the festival's hostesses, carrying fluffy parasols and wearing hoop-skirted dresses and picture hats.

Visitors to Mobile are captivated by its
exciting week-long Mardi Gras celebration (top),
its charming architecture (above), and
beautiful nearby Bellingrath Gardens (left).

The USS *Alabama*, which served in World War II, is moored in Mobile Bay and is open to the public.

Theodore, about 20 miles (32 kilometers) west of Mobile, is the site of Bellingrath Gardens, which features one of the greatest concentrations of azaleas in the South. Flowers bloom in the beautifully landscaped gardens all year round, but the spring show is especially breathtaking.

Mobile's visitor information center is housed in Fort Conde, a reconstruction of the French fort that guarded the city in the eighteenth century.

A gigantic battleship, the USS *Alabama*, is moored at the waterfront of Mobile Bay. Visitors can go aboard and see the historic ship, which was manned by a crew of twenty-five hundred during World War II. The nearby submarine USS *Drum* is also open to the public.

Gulf Shores is a lovely resort on the eastern shore of Mobile Bay.

Lovely beaches are found about 50 miles (80 kilometers) east of Mobile, near Gulf Shores; and on Dauphin Island, about 30 miles (48 kilometers) south of Mobile in the Gulf of Mexico. Gulf State Park is a 6,000-acre (2,428-hectare) playground that includes wide stretches of snow-white sand, a campground, cottages, a motel, a restaurant, and many recreational facilities.

A long, narrow, barrier island lies at the south end of Mobile Bay. Fort Morgan, on its western tip, is a star-shaped brick fort built after the War of 1812. It has been kept in very good condition and is open to the public. Surrounding the fort is Fort Morgan Park, with beaches, fishing piers, and picnic grounds.

The trip from Russell Cave to Huntsville is only about a two-hour drive, but these two places illustrate how Alabama's long history extends from the Stone Age to the Space Age. Alabamians sometimes look at the past with starry-eyed nostalgia, but then they quickly turn their efforts to building the future.

Stars did, indeed, fall on Alabama a century and a half ago, and in the coming century, it is probable that rockets built in the state will be on their way to the stars.

FACTS AT A GLANCE

GENERAL INFORMATION

Statehood: December 14, 1819, twenty-second state

Origin of Name: Alabama is believed to be a rendering of the name of an Indian tribe that once lived in the central part of the state. The name was first given to the principal river of the area. Scholars think that the original word, *Alibamu*, was used to describe the activities of the tribe and meant "thicket clearers" or "vegetation gatherers."

State Capital: Montgomery, founded 1819

State Nickname: "Heart of Dixie," "Cotton State," "Yellowhammer State"

State Flag: The state flag was adopted in 1895 and was patterned after the Confederate battle flag. It shows the red diagonal cross of St. Andrew on a white field, and is edged with gold fringe on three sides.

State Motto: *Audemus Jura Nostra Defendere*, "We dare defend our rights"

State Bird: Yellowhammer

State Fish: Tarpon

State Flower: Camellia

State Mineral: Red iron ore

State Tree: Southern pine

State Song: "Alabama," words by Julia S. Tutwiler; music by Edna Goeckel Gussen:

> Alabama, Alabama
> We will aye be true to thee,
> From thy Southern shore where groweth,
> By the sea thine orange tree.
> To thy Northern vale where floweth,
> Deep and blue thy Tennessee,
> Alabama, Alabama,
> We will aye be true to thee!

The Japanese Gardens in Birmingham

Broad the Stream whose name thou bearest;
Grand thy Bigbee rolls along;
Fair thy Coosa—Tailapoosa
Bold thy Warrior, dark and strong,
Goodlier than the land that Moses
Climbed lone Nebo's Mount to see,
Alabama, Alabama,
We will aye be true to thee!

From thy prairies broad and fertile,
Where thy snow-white cotton shines,
To the hills where coal and iron
Hide in thy exhaustless mines,
Strong-armed miners—sturdy farmers:
Loyal hearts what'er we be,
Alabama, Alabama,
We will aye be true to thee!

From the quarries where the marble
White as that of Paros gleams
Waiting till thy sculptor's chisel,
Wake to life thy poet's dreams;
For not only wealth of nature,
Wealth of mind hast thou to see,
Alabama, Alabama,
We will aye be true to thee!

Where the perfumed south wind whispers,
Thy magnolia groves among,
Softer than a mother's kisses,
Sweeter than a mother's song;
Where the golden jasmine trailing
Woos the treasure-laden bee,
Alabama, Alabama
We will aye be true to thee!

Brave and pure thy men and women
Better this than corn and wine,
Make us worthy, God in Heaven,
Of this goodly land of Thine,
Hearts as open as our doorways,
Liberal hands and spirits free,
Alabama, Alabama,
We will aye be true to thee!

Little, little, can I give thee,
Alabama, mother mine;
But that little—hand, brain, spirit,
All I have and am are thine,
Take, O take the gift and giver,
Take and serve thyself with me,
Alabama, Alabama,
I will aye be true to thee!

Mardi Gras celebration in Mobile

POPULATION

Population: 3,893,978, twenty-second among the states (1980 census)

Population Density: 75 people per sq. mi. (29 people per km^2)

Population Distribution: About 62 percent of Alabama's population is urban; 38 percent is rural. One-fourth of the people in the state live in its ten largest cities, and about 17 percent of the people live in the four largest cities—Birmingham, Mobile, Montgomery, and Huntsville.

Birmingham	286,799
Mobile	200,452
Montgomery	177,857
Huntsville	142,513
Tuscaloosa	75,211
Dothan	48,750
Gadsden	47,565
Decatur	42,002
Prichard	39,546
Florence	37,029

Population Growth:

Year	Population
1820	127,901
1830	309,527
1840	590,756
1850	771,623
1860	964,201
1870	996,992
1880	1,262,505
1890	1,513,401
1900	1,828,697
1910	2,138,093
1920	2,348,174
1930	2,646,248
1940	2,832,961
1950	3,061,743
1960	3,266,740
1970	3,444,354
1980	3,893,978

GEOGRAPHY

Borders: Alabama is bordered on the north by Tennessee, on the east by Georgia, on the south by Florida and the Gulf of Mexico, and on the west by Mississippi.

Highest Point: Cheaha Mountain in Cleburne County, 2,407 ft. (734 m)

Lowest Point: Sea level, along the Gulf of Mexico

Greatest Distances: East to west—210 mi. (338 km)
North to south—329 mi. (530 km)

Area: 51,705 sq. mi. (133,915 km²)

Rank in Area Among the States: Twenty-ninth

Rivers: There are approximately 1,600 mi. (2,575 km) of navigable waterways in Alabama. The Mobile River, which flows southward into the Gulf of Mexico and is part of the most important river system in the state, is formed by the confluence of the Tombigbee and Alabama rivers. The Perdido River, which also flows into the Gulf of Mexico, forms part of the border between Alabama and Florida. The Alabama is fed by the Cahaba, Coosa, and Tallapoosa rivers. The chief tributary of the Tombigbee is the Black Warrior River. The Tennessee River snakes westward across the northern part of the state. The Chattahoochee, which forms part of the Alabama-Georgia border, drains the southeastern part of the state.

A herd of cattle near Eufaula in southeastern Alabama

Lakes: All the large lakes in the state have been formed by the construction of electric-power dams. Guntersville Lake, formed by the Guntersville Dam on the Tennessee River, is the largest, covering 110 sq. mi. (285 km²). Other large man-made lakes include Pickwick, Wheeler, and Wilson lakes on the Tennessee River; Weiss Lake on the Coosa River; Martin Lake on the Tallapoosa River; and Lake Eufaula on the Chattahoochee River.

Topography: Coastal plains cover most of southern Alabama. Most of the southern half of the state lies less than 500 ft. (152 m) above sea level. Toward the north, the terrain becomes more varied, with gently rolling land and low hills. The state can be divided into six land regions.

The Interior Low Plateau, in the northwest part of the state, is an area of rich agricultural land. Much of the region lies in the valley of the Tennessee River. The Cumberland Plateau slopes from the hilly northeastern corner of Alabama to the primarily flat land in the center of the state. The soil here is sandy. The Appalachian Ridge and Valley Region, southeast of the Cumberland Plateau, is an area rich in such minerals as coal, iron, and limestone. The Piedmont Region consists of low hills and ridges and sandy valleys, and has deposits of coal, iron, marble, and limestone. It is located in the east-central part of the state and is an important manufacturing area. Cheaha Mountain, the highest point in the state, is located here. The East Gulf Coastal Plain, the state's largest region, covers most of the southern two-thirds of the state. Although the soil of the western part of this region is too sandy and gravelly for growing crops, the southeastern section of the

Bathers on Alabama's Gulf coast

region is very fertile and is an important farming area. Pine forests cover much of the northern part of the region. The southwestern part of the region is made up of the low, swampy land of the Mobile River Delta. The Black Belt is a strip of prairie land that cuts into the East Gulf Coastal Plain in the south-central part of the state. The area is named for its rich, black soil. Although cotton plantations once dominated this fertile area, the land is now used largely for raising livestock.

Climate: Summers in Alabama are long and hot; winters are generally mild. In the winter, temperatures average about 46° F. (8° C) in the north and about 52° F. (11° C) in the south. Summer temperatures average about 80° F. (27° C) statewide. Snow falls in the northern region but is rare in the southern coastal areas. Alabama's annual precipitation ranges from an average of 65 in. (165 cm) on the coast to 53 in. (135 cm) in the north. Although rainfall is usually abundant in all parts of the state throughout the year, droughts sometimes occur. The lowest temperature recorded in the state was -27° F. (-33° C) at New Market on January 30, 1966. The highest temperature recorded was 112° F. (44° C) at Centreville on September 5, 1925.

NATURE

Trees: Loblolly pine, shortleaf pine, longleaf pine, slash pine, red oak, white oak, hickory, cedar, cypress, hemlock, black gum, sweet gum, tupelo gum, yellow poplar

Wild Plants: Azaleas, mountain laurels, rhododendrons, orchids, wild roses, Johnny-jump-ups, lilies, wild hydrangeas, asters, Dutchman's-breeches, goldenrods, orchids, pinks, southern camasses, ageratum, jack-in-the-pulpits, yarrow, yucca

Animals: Minks, raccoons, muskrats, nutrias, flying squirrels, grey squirrels, fox squirrels, mice, bats, red and gray foxes, opossums, bobcats, rabbits, white-tailed deer, skunks, black bears, beavers, alligators; numerous kinds of snakes, toads, frogs, salamanders, lizards, and turtles

Birds: Mallards and other kinds of ducks, wild turkeys, hawks, turkey buzzards, great horned owls, golden eagles, ospreys, herons, yellowhammers, whippoorwills, flycatchers, warblers, blue jays, crows, robins, cardinals, sparrows, swallows, swifts, goldfinches, mockingbirds, thrashers, woodpeckers, bobwhites

Fish: Freshwater fish in Alabama include bream, shad, catfish, carp, crappie, drumfish, and bass; along the Gulf coast one can find tarpon, pompano, dolphin, mackerel, red snapper, king mackerel, bluefish, bonita, sturgeon, redfish, and mullet.

GOVERNMENT

Alabama is governed under a constitution that was adopted in 1901; the document has had more than 440 amendments. The state government of Alabama, like the federal government, is made up of three branches: legislative, executive, and judicial. The state legislature has two houses—a senate with 35 members and a house of representatives with 105 members. The legislature creates new laws, rescinds or revises old ones, and works with the governor to prepare the state budget. Both senators and representatives are elected to four-year terms.

The executive branch, headed by the governor, executes the law. The governor may serve an unlimited number of four-year terms, but cannot serve more than two terms in succession. The governor has the authority to veto or approve laws passed by the legislature, to grant pardons, to serve as commander-in-chief of the state militia, and to call emergency sessions of the legislature.

The judicial branch interprets the law and tries cases. The state's highest court, the state supreme court, has a chief justice and eight associate justices. Alabama also has a court of criminal appeals with five judges, and a civil-appeals court with three judges. All of these judges are elected to six-year terms. The state has several lower courts, including circuit, district, probate, and municipal courts.

Number of Counties: 67

U.S. Representatives: 7

Electoral Votes: 9

Voting Qualifications: All properly registered United States citizens eighteen years of age or over are qualified to vote in Alabama.

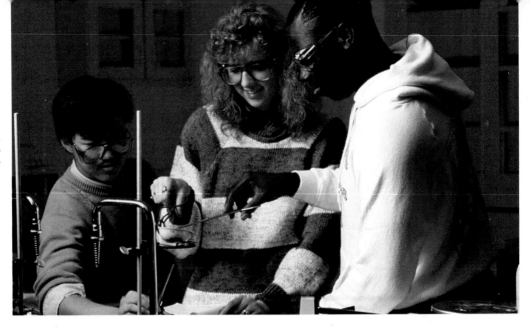

A high-school chemistry class in Mobile

EDUCATION

The Alabama state public-school system was established in 1854. The superintendent, appointed by the state board of education, is the head of the state's public-school system. Policies are established by a nine-member board of education. Children between the ages of seven and fifteen are required by state law to attend school.

Alabama has about sixty institutions of higher learning. Thirty-seven of these are public colleges or universities. The University of Alabama, the state's largest university, was founded in 1831. It has campuses in University (a section of Tuscaloosa), Birmingham, and Huntsville. Auburn University, another large state-supported school, has campuses at Auburn and Montgomery. Other state schools include Troy State University, with campuses in Troy and Montgomery; the University of North Alabama, in Florence; the University of South Alabama, in Mobile; Jacksonville State University; Livingston University; and the University of Montevallo. Samford University and Birmingham-Southern College in Birmingham, Spring Hill College in Mobile, Tuskegee University, and Huntingdon College in Montgomery are among the private schools in Alabama.

ECONOMY AND INDUSTRY

Principal Products:

Agriculture: Soybeans, peanuts, corn, wheat, cotton, vegetables, pecans, poultry, dairy cattle, hogs, fish

Manufacturing: Clothing, textiles, lumber and wood products, paper and allied products, rubber and plastics products, primary metals, food products, chemicals and allied products

Natural Resources: Coal, oil, natural gas, dolomite, graphite, bauxite, marble, sandstone, sand and gravel, clays, limestone

Hay is an important Alabama field crop.

Business and Industry: Manufacturing is the single most-important economic activity in Alabama, making up about one-fourth of the gross state product (the total value of all goods and services produced annually in a state). The low-cost electrical power made possible by TVA dams on the Tennessee River has encouraged heavy industry in the area. The service industries of the state's ten largest cities make up about two-thirds of the gross state product. The leading retail businesses in the state are automotive sales, food stores, and general merchandise stores. Shipping is an important aspect of the state's economy. The port of Mobile is an important distribution point for coal and petroleum products. Tourism brings more than $3 billion to the state's economy every year.

Communication: About 100 newspapers are published in Alabama, and about 30 of these are dailies. The state's oldest newspaper, founded in 1813, is the *Mobile Register*. The *Birmingham News* has the largest circulation in the state. The *Birmingham Post-Herald*, the *Montgomery Advertiser*, and the *Huntsville Times* are other widely read papers. *Southern Living*, based in Birmingham, is a highly successful regional magazine.

Alabama has about 154 AM and 87 FM radio stations and about 25 television stations. The State Educational Television Commission operates 9 of the television stations. In 1955, the state established the Alabama Public Television Network, the nation's first state-owned educational television system. Cable television systems serve more than half a million subscribers in Alabama.

The George Washington Carver Museum, on the campus of Tuskegee University, celebrates the contributions blacks have made to American history and culture.

Transportation: Alabama has about 97,000 mi. (156,106 km) of roads and highways and about 4,500 mi. (7,242 km) of railroad track. Four major interstate highways cross the state. I-10 passes through Mobile as it cuts across the southwestern tip of the state. I-85 runs northeast from Montgomery toward Atlanta, Georgia. I-65 is a north-south route that begins in Mobile and runs up the middle of the state. I-59, which runs diagonally across the state, is the major route between Jackson, Mississippi, and Chattanooga, Tennessee.

About 1,350 mi. (2,173 km) of navigable waterways cross the state. Major navigable waterways are the Tennessee-Tombigbee system and the Black Warrior, Mobile, Alabama, and Chattahoochee rivers. Airports with scheduled passenger service are located at Anniston, Auburn, Birmingham, Dothan, Gadsden, Huntsville, Mobile, Montgomery, Muscle Shoals, and Tuscaloosa.

SOCIAL AND CULTURAL LIFE

Museums: Alabama has approximately sixty museums. The state's most popular museum is the Alabama Space and Rocket Center in Huntsville. Art museums in the state include the Museum of Art in Birmingham, the Mobile Art Gallery, and the Museum of Fine Arts in Montgomery. Specialized museums in the state include the George Washington Carver Museum in Tuskegee, the Edith Nourse Rogers Museum at the U.S. Women's Army Corps Center at Fort McClellan, the Regar

The Birmingham Public Library is the state's largest library.

Museum of Natural History in Anniston, the United States Army Aviation Museum at Fort Rucker, and the Museum of the City of Mobile.

Libraries: There are about two hundred public libraries in the state, including municipal, county, and regional libraries. The Birmingham Public Library is the state's largest library. Mobile, Huntsville, and Montgomery also have large libraries. In all, the Alabama public library system has nearly 6 million volumes. The Alabama Department of History and Archives Library in Montgomery houses special collections about the state. The Amelia Gale Gorgas Library at the University of Alabama in Tuscaloosa has a wide variety of materials on the history of the region. Rare medical books are housed at the Lawrence Reynolds Library at the University of Alabama Medical Center in Birmingham. The Alabama Space and Rocket Center has an extensive collection of materials on aviation and space exploration.

Performing Arts: The Alabama Shakespeare Festival in Montgomery is one of North America's finest theater complexes. On the same grounds is the Montgomery Museum of Fine Arts. The Alabama Symphony Orchestra, based in

A young fisherman displays his catch at Fairhope Pier.

Birmingham, is the state's only professional symphony; Huntsville and Montgomery have volunteer orchestras. Birmingham has an opera company and a professional ballet company.

Sports and Recreation: College football is the state's most popular spectator sport. The teams of the University of Alabama and Auburn University are consistently rated among the top ten college teams and have won many honors. Birmingham has a minor-league baseball club. Stock-car races are held at the Alabama International Motor Speedway in Talladega. During spring and summer, horse shows are held in Anniston, Athens, and Guntersville.

Lovers of the outdoors can enjoy the state's twenty-four state parks and four national forests. William B. Bankhead National Forest, located in the northwestern part of the state, is a scenic region of lakes, streams, canyons, waterfalls, and large stands of hardwood trees. Talladega National Forest has two separate sections: Oakmulgee, in the west-central part of the state; and Talladega, in northeastern Alabama. Cheaha Mountain, the highest point in the state, lies in the Oakmulgee section of Talladega National Forest. Tuskegee National Forest lies in east-central

Birmingham has a minor-league baseball club, the red-uniformed Birmingham Barons.

Alabama, and Conecuh Forest straddles the Alabama-Florida border. Alabama's coastal area, as well as its many rivers, streams, and lakes, provide unlimited opportunities for fishing, boating, and swimming.

Historic Sites and Landmarks:

Battleship Park, east of Mobile, features tours of the USS *Alabama*, a battleship used in World War II and the Korean conflict. Also on display are the submarine USS *Drum* and several World War II aircraft.

Dexter Avenue King Memorial Baptist Church, in Montgomery, was the pastorate of Dr. Martin Luther King, Jr., from 1954 to 1960. It has been designated a National Historic Landmark.

First White House of the Confederacy, in Montgomery, was the residence of Confederate president Jefferson Davis during the first few months of the Civil War.

Fort Conde, in Mobile, is a reconstruction of an eighteenth-century French fort.

Fort Morgan, near Gulf Shores, was one of the forts from which Confederate forces tried to defend Mobile Bay during the Civil War.

Horseshoe Bend National Military Park, near Dadeville, was the site of the battle that ended the Creek Indian War of 1813-14. General Andrew Jackson's decisive victory here helped spur his military and political career.

Russell Cave housed Alabama's earliest-known human inhabitants.

Mound State Monument, in Moundville, was a prehistoric Indian settlement and ceremonial center. It includes some forty ceremonial mounds, a reconstructed Indian village, and a museum that features excavated Indian burials.

Old North Hull Historic District, in Montgomery, consists of several restored nineteenth-century buildings.

Russell Cave National Monument, near Bridgeport, is a cave that housed the earliest-known human inhabitants of Alabama. The site is unusual in that it was inhabited continuously over an eight-thousand-year period, beginning about 7000 B.C.

Sloss Furnaces, in Birmingham, is a complex of hundred-year-old iron furnaces that has been converted into an industrial museum and auditorium.

State Capitol, in Montgomery, is a Greek Revival-style building decorated with colorful murals depicting the state's history.

Tannehill Historical State Park, near Bessemer, was the birthplace of Alabama's iron and steel industry. The Tannehill Ironworks produced pig iron for the Confederacy. A village museum has been created around the ruins of the furnaces.

Tuskegee Institute National Historic Site, in Tuskegee, includes the campus of Tuskegee University, Booker T. Washington's home, and the George Washington Carver Museum.

The Ave Maria Grotto in Cullman features 150 tiny replicas of cathedrals and churches from all over the world.

Other Interesting Places to Visit:

Alabama Space and Rocket Center, in Huntsville, is the world's largest space museum; displays, films, and exhibits interpret the history of the space program.

Ave Maria Grotto, in Cullman, is a 4-acre (1.6-hectare) site that contains more than 150 miniature replicas of famous churches and shrines from all over the world.

Bellingrath Gardens, in Theodore, contains some of the most beautiful formal gardens in the world. It is especially known for its spectacular array of azaleas.

Birmingham Zoo, in Birmingham, is the largest zoo in the southeastern United States.

Discovery Place, in Birmingham, is a museum that features "hands-on" science, arts, and technical exhibits.

Indian Mound and Museum, in Florence, is the site of the largest ceremonial Indian mound in the Tennessee River Valley. The archaeological museum at the base of the mound has a large collection of Indian artifacts.

A bust of Helen Keller and the pump where she learned her first word are on display at Ivy Green, the birthplace of the famous lecturer and author.

Ivy Green, in Tuscumbia, is the birthplace of Helen Keller.

Oak Mountain State Park, in Birmingham, is one of the most scenic areas in the state, featuring two lakes, rugged mountains, a gorge, and waterfalls.

United States Army Aviation Museum, near Ozark, includes early army aircraft, helicopters, and other items related to aviation.

W.C. Handy Home and Museum, in Florence, is the restored birthplace of William C. Handy, the jazz composer known as the "father of the blues."

IMPORTANT DATES

1519—Spanish explorer Alonso Álvarez de Piñeda sails into Mobile Bay

1528—Spanish explorer Pánfilo de Narváez arrives at Mobile Bay

1540—Hernando De Soto explores much of the area now known as Alabama

1559—Spaniard Tristán de Luna, seeking gold, starts a temporary settlement on Mobile Bay

1702—French settlers led by Pierre Le Moyne, Sieur d'Iberville, and his brother Jean Baptiste Le Moyne, Sieur de Bienville, found Fort Louis de la Mobile on the Mobile River

Fort Conde, established by the French in the early 1700s, has been partially reconstructed.

1711—Floods force the French settlers to move south to the site of present-day Mobile

1720—Fort Louis de la Mobile is renamed Fort Conde de la Mobile

1722—The capital of French Louisiana is moved from Fort Conde de la Mobile to New Orleans

1763—By the Treaty of Paris ending the French and Indian War, France cedes the land that makes up present-day Alabama to Great Britain

1780—Spain captures Mobile from the British

1783—By the Treaty of Paris ending the American Revolution, Britain cedes northern Alabama to the United States and cedes the Mobile region to Spain

1813—The United States seizes the Mobile region from Spain; Creek Indians raid Fort Mims

1814—General Andrew Jackson and his troops defeat the Creek Indians in the Battle of Horseshoe Bend; the Creeks surrender their lands to the United States

1817—Congress organizes the Alabama Territory

1819—Alabama is admitted to the Union as the twenty-second state

1833—"Stars fall on Alabama" during a meteor shower

1837—Alabama's economy is severely affected by a nationwide economic panic

1843—Alabama state bank fails

1846—Montgomery becomes the state capital

1861—Alabama secedes from the Union, exists briefly as the Republic of Alabama, then joins the Confederate States of America

1864—After a fierce naval struggle, the Battle of Mobile Bay is won by Union forces

1868—Alabama is readmitted into the Union

1871—Birmingham is founded

1880—Alabama's first blast furnace (to process iron ore) is opened in Birmingham

1881—Booker T. Washington establishes the Tuskegee Normal and Industrial Institute

1886—The nation's first city-wide electric trolley system begins operating in Montgomery

1888—First Alabama steel is produced in North Birmingham and Bessemer

1890s—The manufacture of iron and steel products becomes the state's most important industry

1901—Present state constitution is adopted

1928—The convict lease-system is abolished

1933—Congress creates the Tennessee Valley Authority

1940s—During World War II, Redstone Arsenal is established at Huntsville; Alabama becomes a major arsenal, air-force training field, and shipbuilding center

1944—Alabama's first oil field is discovered at Gilbertown

1955—Montgomery bus rider Rosa Parks is arrested for not giving up her seat to a white person; Montgomery's blacks, led by Dr. Martin Luther King, Jr., stage a year-long bus boycott

1956—Montgomery is ordered to desegregate its public bus system

1960—NASA opens the George C. Marshall Space Flight Center at Huntsville

1965—Martin Luther King, Jr. leads more than twenty-five thousand people on a march from Selma to Montgomery to protest voter discrimination; the march leads to passage of the Voting Rights Act of 1965

1970—The Alabama Space and Rocket Center is established in Huntsville

1972—Alabama governor George Wallace is shot while campaigning in New Jersey for the presidency of the United States

1974—George Wallace becomes the first Alabama governor to be elected for a third term

1982—George Wallace is elected governor of Alabama for a fourth term

1985—The Alabama Shakespeare Festival opens in its new home in Montgomery

1986—Guy Hunt becomes the first Republican governor of Alabama since the Reconstruction era

IMPORTANT PEOPLE

HENRY AARON

Henry Louis (Hank) Aaron (1934-   ), born in Mobile; professional baseball player; broke Babe Ruth's record for career home runs by hitting his 755th run on April 8, 1974; played twenty-one seasons in the major leagues with a lifetime batting average of .310 and 2,202 runs batted in; awarded the Spingarn Medal by the National Association for the Advancement of Colored People (NAACP) (1974)

John Hollis Bankhead (1842-1920), politician; served in the Confederate forces and entered public service in 1865; U.S. representative (1887-1907); U.S. senator (1907-20); helped develop the first national automobile highway system and the first transcontinental highway; pioneered legislation that led to the Tennessee River flood-control and transportation system

John Hollis Bankhead, Jr. (1872-1946), born in Moscow; politician; son of John Hollis Bankhead; U.S. senator (1930-46); coauthored the Bankhead Cotton Control Act, which created federal authority over farm productivity for the first time in American history

Tallulah Brockman Bankhead (1903-1968), born in Huntsville; actress; daughter of William Brockman Bankhead; leading stage and motion picture actress known for her husky voice and air of sophistication

TALLULAH BANKHEAD

HUGO BLACK

GEORGE W. CARVER

NAT KING COLE

J.L.M. CURRY

William Brockman Bankhead (1874-1940), born in Moscow; politician; U.S. representative (1917-40); Speaker of the House (1936-40)

William Wyatt Bibb (1781-1820), physician, politician; first territorial governor of Alabama (1817-18); first state governor of Alabama (1819-20)

Hugo Lafayette Black (1886-1971), born in Harlan; politician, jurist; U.S. senator (1927-37), associate justice of the U.S. Supreme Court (1937-71); known for supporting government protection of civil rights; served one of the longest terms in the history of the court

Winton "Red" Blount (1921-   ), Montgomery construction and manufacturing executive; U.S. postmaster general (1969-71)

Paul "Bear" Bryant (1913-1983), head football coach at the University of Alabama (1958-82); considered one of America's greatest college football coaches; earned 323 victories in his thirty-eight-year career; had three undefeated seasons and nine in which his team lost only one game; took twenty teams to major bowl games

George Washington Carver (1864-1943), botanist, educator; won international fame for his work in agricultural research; director of the Department of Agricultural Research at Tuskegee Institute (1896-1943); developed hundreds of products from peanuts and sweet potatoes; won numerous awards for his accomplishments, including the NAACP Spingarn Medal (1923) and the Theodore Roosevelt Medal (1939); gave his life savings to establish the Carver Foundation for research in creative chemistry

Nathaniel Adams (Nat King) Cole (1919-1965), born in Montgomery; musician, singer; soloist and leader of the King Cole Trio, a successful jazz trio (1939-51); in the 1940s, was the only black performer to have his own commercial network radio program; in 1956 became the first black entertainer to have his own national television show; produced many hit records and received numerous awards

Braxton Bragg Comer (1848-1927), politician; governor of Alabama (1907-11); known as Alabama's "Education Governor"; built a county high school in every county in the state; had new buildings constructed at the University of Alabama, Auburn University, and other colleges

Jabez Lamar Monroe Curry (1825-1903), politician, diplomat, and educator; U.S. representative (1857-61); member of the Confederate Congress (1861-63, 1864); served in Confederate army during the Civil War; president of Howard College (now Samford University) (1865-68); U.S. minister to Spain (1885-88, 1902); worked throughout his life to make education possible for all children, black and white, in the South; a statue of him stands in Statuary Hall in the U.S. Capitol in Washington, D.C.

Louise Fletcher (1936-   ), born in Birmingham; actress; won the Academy Award for Best Actress for her role in *One Flew Over the Cuckoo's Nest* (1975)

William Crawford Gorgas (1854-1920), born in Mobile; physician; was known as the world's leading sanitation expert; surgeon general of the U.S. Army; pioneer in the elimination of yellow fever, malaria, and the bubonic plague

William Christopher (W. C.) Handy (1873-1958), born in Florence; musician and composer; known as the "father of the blues"; known for such songs as "St. Louis Blues," "Beale Street Blues," and "Memphis Blues"

John William Heisman (1869-1936), football coach; coached at Auburn University (1895-1903); helped revolutionize the rules and strategy of the game of football; the Heisman Trophy, given annually to the best college football player in the nation, is named for him

Joseph (Lister) Hill (1894-1984), born in Montgomery; physician, politician; U.S. senator (1938-69); distinguished for his work in health-care legislation, including the Hill-Burton Act; recipient of awards from such organizations as the American Hospital Association, the National Academy of Sciences, and the National Conference of Christians and Jews

Joseph Henry Johnson (1832-1893), social worker and educator; founder of the Alabama Institute for Deaf and Blind

Helen Adams Keller (1880-1968), born in Tuscumbia; author and lecturer; lost both her sight and hearing before the age of two; learned to communicate with the help of her teacher, Anne Sullivan; graduated from Radcliffe College with honors; became internationally known for her work on behalf of the handicapped; recipient of numerous awards for her remarkable achievements

Martin Luther King, Jr. (1929-1968), clergyman, civil-rights leader; advocated demonstrating for social change through nonviolent means; while serving as pastor of the Dexter Avenue Baptist Church in Montgomery, led the 1955 Montgomery bus boycott to protest segregation in public places; in 1957, organized the Southern Christian Leadership Conference, a civil-rights organization; as the leader of the Civil Rights Movement of the 1960s, led numerous peaceful marches and protests to end racial discrimination, including the 1965 march from Selma to Montgomery to protest voter discrimination; his efforts led to such victories as passage of the Civil Rights Act of 1964 and the Voting Rights Act of 1965; awarded the Nobel Peace Prize (1964); assassinated in 1968 in Memphis

Coretta Scott King (1927-   ), born near Marion; civil-rights leader; widow of Martin Luther King, Jr.; continued the work of her husband after his death; president of the Martin Luther King, Jr. Center for Social Change in Atlanta

LOUISE FLETCHER

WILLIAM GORGAS

HELEN KELLER

MARTIN LUTHER KING, JR.

WILLIAM RUFUS KING

HARPER LEE

WILLIE MAYS

ROSA PARKS

William Rufus Devane King (1786-1853), politician; member of the constitutional convention that drafted Alabama's first constitution; U.S. senator (1819-44, 1848-52); minister to France (1844-46); vice-president of the United States (1853)

Nelle (Harper) Lee (1926-   ), born in Monroeville; novelist; Alabama's most distinguished author; received the 1961 Pulitzer Prize in fiction for her novel *To Kill a Mockingbird*, a moving story that takes place in a small Alabama town

Joe Louis (1914-1981), born Joe Louis Barrow in Lafayette; professional boxer; known as the "Brown Bomber"; world heavyweight boxing champion (1937-49); won sixty-eight of the seventy-one contests of his professional career

Willie Howard Mays (1931-   ), born in Westfield; professional baseball player; played with the New York (later San Francisco) Giants and the New York Mets; during his twenty-two-year career, hit 660 home runs, led the National League in home runs four times and in stolen bases four times, and was twice named the league's Most Valuable Player (1954, 1965); elected to the Baseball Hall of Fame (1979)

Alexander McGillivray (1759?-1793), born near present-day Montgomery; Creek Indian leader born of a Scottish father and a French-Creek mother; worked to unite the Creek people and protect Indian lands from American settlers

John Hunt Morgan (1825-1864), born in Huntsville; military officer; served in the Mexican War; Confederate general who was famous for his cavalry raids in Kentucky and Tennessee during the Civil War

James Cleveland (Jesse) Owens (1913-1980), born in Oakville; world-champion track-and-field athlete; winner of four gold medals at the 1936 Olympic games in Berlin

Leroy (Satchel) Paige (1906-1982), born in Mobile; professional baseball player; one of the greatest pitchers of all time; played in segregated black leagues (1924-47); is said to have won 104 of 105 games in 1934; pitched for the Cleveland Indians (1948-49), St. Louis Browns (1951-53), and Kansas City Athletics (1965); pitched at least fifty-five career no-hitters; elected to the Baseball Hall of Fame (1971)

Rosa Parks (1913-   ), born in Tuskegee; became famous after she was arrested for refusing to give up her seat to a white person on a crowded bus in Montgomery in 1955; the incident led to the historic Montgomery bus boycott and helped bring about the Civil Rights Movement; for her work in civil rights, was awarded the NAACP's Spingarn Medal (1979)

Lionel Ritchie (1950-   ), born in Tuskegee; singer, composer, musician, producer; has won numerous Grammy awards; his *Can't Slow Down* is the largest-selling album in the history of Motown Records

Raphael Semmes (1809-1877), naval officer; during the Civil War, commanded the famous Confederate commerce destroyer *Alabama* (1862-64); practiced law in Mobile (1867-77)

John Jackson Sparkman (1899-1985), born near Hartselle; politician; U.S. representative (1937-46), U.S. senator, (1946-79); Democratic nominee for vice-president in 1952

Benjamin Sterling Turner (1825-1894), politician; first black U.S. representative from Alabama (1871-73)

Tuskalusa (?-?), Choctaw Indian chief; he and his warriors were defeated by Hernando De Soto and his men after they attacked the Indian village of Mabila in 1540; the city and county of Tuscaloosa are named for him

Julia Strudwick Tutwiler (1841-1916), born in Tuscaloosa; educator and social reformer; helped establish several girls' schools and campaigned successfully for the admission of women to the University of Alabama; worked for prison reform; wrote the words to "Alabama," the Alabama state song

Robert Jemison Van de Graaff (1901-1967), born in Tuscaloosa; physicist; inventor of the electrostatic generator, a device used in nuclear research

George Corley Wallace (1919-   ), born in Clio; lawyer, politician; assistant attorney general of Alabama (1946-47); member of the Alabama legislature (1947-53); Alabama state judge (1953-58); governor of Alabama (1963-66, 1971-79, 1983-87); during his first term as governor, became known for his opposition to school integration and his support of states' rights; American Independent Party nominee for president in 1968; in 1972, while campaigning for the Democratic presidential nomination, was shot and seriously wounded by a would-be assassin; won his fourth term as governor by promising to address the problems of all Alabamians, both black and white

Lurleen Burns Wallace (1926-68), born in Tuscaloosa; wife of George Wallace; first woman governor of Alabama (1967-68); because Alabama law (at the time) prohibited her husband from seeking two gubernatorial terms in a row, she was elected with the understanding that her husband would continue to set state policy; died while in office

Booker Taliaferro Washington (1856-1915), lecturer, author, and educator; held the conservative view that blacks needed to make educational and economic progress before attempting to demand civil and political rights; was born a slave in Virginia; was educated at and later taught at Hampton Institute in Virginia; in 1881 was chosen to organize Tuskegee Institute, a school for blacks that emphasized practical, vocational training; president of Tuskegee Institute (1881-1915); organized the National Negro Business League

JOHN SPARKMAN

JULIA TUTWILER

GEORGE WALLACE

BOOKER T. WASHINGTON

WILLIAM YANCEY

Dinah Washington (1924-1967), born in Tuscaloosa; noted jazz and blues singer and pianist

Joseph Wheeler (1836-1906), army officer, politician; known as "Fighting Joe," he was one of the Confederacy's most illustrious officers; U.S. representative from Alabama (1881-82, 1883, 1885-1900)

Hank Williams (1923-1953), born near Georgiana; country and western singer and composer; helped popularize country music; popular performer at the Grand Ole Opry; composed more than 125 songs, including his famous "Cold, Cold Heart"

William Lowndes Yancey (1814-1863), politician; U.S. representative (1844-46); known as "The Orator of Secession" because of his strong advocacy of states' rights; prepared Alabama's Secession Ordinance; Confederate commissioner to England and France (1861-62); Confederate senator (1862-63)

GOVERNORS

William Wyatt Bibb	1819-1820	Thomas Goode Jones	1890-1894
Thomas Bibb	1820-1821	William Calvin Oates	1894-1896
Israel Pickens	1821-1825	Joseph Forney Johnston	1896-1900
John Murphy	1825-1829	William James Samford	1900-1901
Gabriel Moore	1829-1831	William Dorsey Jelks	1901-1907
Samuel B. Moore	1831	Braxton Bragg Comer	1907-1911
John Gayle	1831-1835	Emmett O'Neal	1911-1915
Clement Comer Clay	1835-1837	Charles Henderson	1915-1919
Hugh McVay	1837	Thomas Erby Kilby	1919-1923
Arthur Pendleton Bagby	1837-1841	William Woodward Brandon	1923-1927
Benjamin Fitzpatrick	1841-1845	Bibb Graves	1927-1931
Joshua Lanier Martin	1845-1847	Benjamin Meek Miller	1931-1935
Reuben Chapman	1847-1849	Bibb Graves	1935-1939
Henry Watkins Collier	1849-1853	Frank M. Dixon	1939-1942
John Anthony Winston	1853-1857	Chauncey Sparks	1942-1947
Andrew Barry Moore	1857-1861	James E. Folsom	1947-1951
John Gill Shorter	1861-1863	Gordon Persons	1951-1955
Thomas Hill Watts	1863-1865	James E. Folsom	1955-1959
Lewis E. Parsons	1865	John M. Patterson	1959-1963
Robert Miller Patton	1865-1867	George C. Wallace	1963-1967
(military rule)	1867-1868	Lurleen B. Wallace	1967-1968
William Hugh Smith	1868-1870	Albert P. Brewer	1968-1971
Robert Burns Lindsay	1870-1872	George C. Wallace	1971-1979
David Peter Lewis	1872-1874	Forrest Hood James, Jr.	1979-1983
George Smith Houston	1874-1878	George C. Wallace	1983-1987
Rufus W. Cobb	1878-1882	Guy Hunt	1987-
Edward Asbury O'Neal	1882-1886		
Thomas Seay	1886-1890		

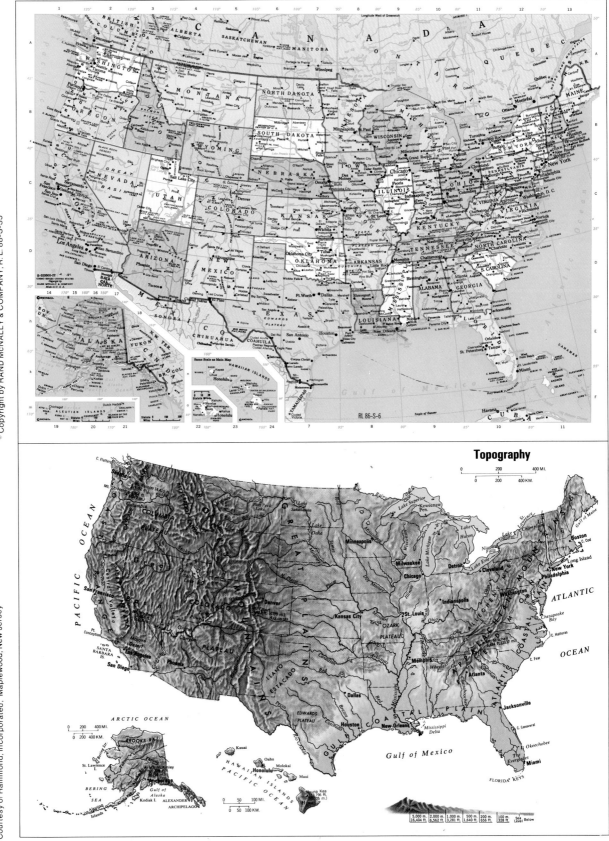

Topography

MAP KEY

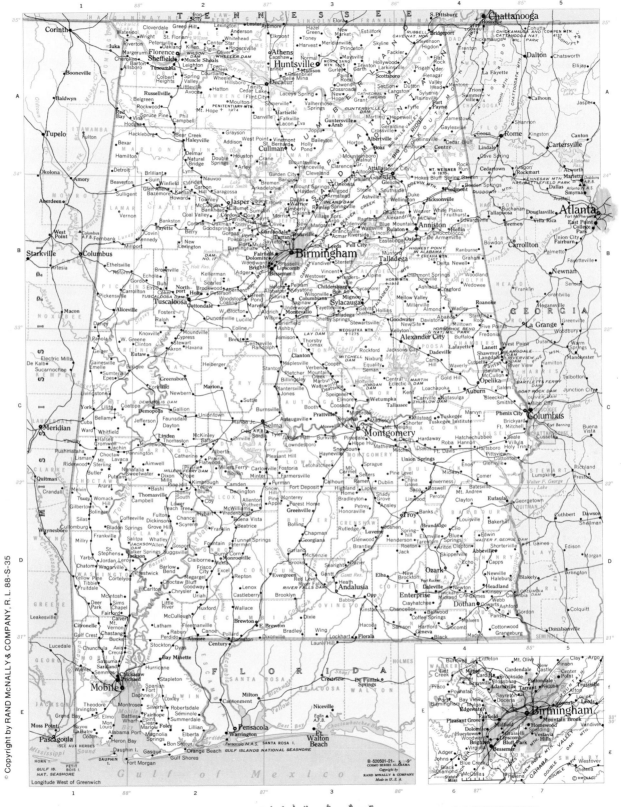

Statute Miles

Kilometers

Lambert Conformal Conic Projection

B-520501-21—-9"
COSMO SERIES ALABAMA
Copyright by
RAND McNALLY & COMPANY
Made in U.S.A.

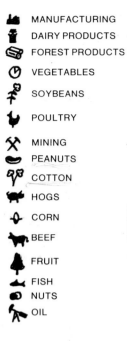

MANUFACTURING
DAIRY PRODUCTS
FOREST PRODUCTS
VEGETABLES
SOYBEANS
POULTRY
MINING
PEANUTS
COTTON
HOGS
CORN
BEEF
FRUIT
FISH
NUTS
OIL

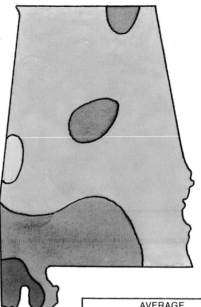

AVERAGE
YEARLY
PRECIPITATION

Centimeters		Inches
163 to 183		64 to 72
142 to 163		56 to 64
122 to 142		48 to 56
102 to 122		40 to 48

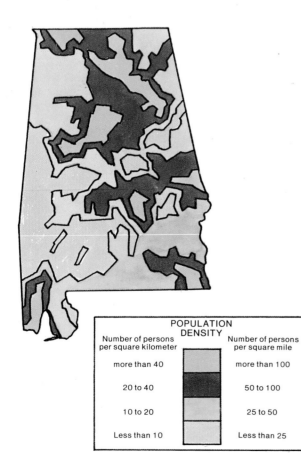

POPULATION
DENSITY

Number of persons per square kilometer		Number of persons per square mile
more than 40		more than 100
20 to 40		50 to 100
10 to 20		25 to 50
Less than 10		Less than 25

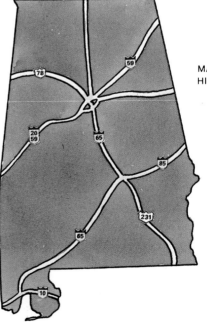

MAJOR
HIGHWAYS

TOPOGRAPHY

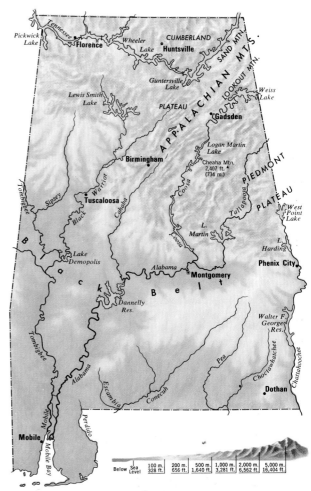

Cheaha Mtn.
2,407 ft.
(734 m.)

Courtesy of Hammond, Incorporated
Maplewood, New Jersey

Below Sea Level | 100 m. 328 ft. | 200 m. 656 ft. | 500 m. 1,640 ft. | 1,000 m. 3,281 ft. | 2,000 m. 6,562 ft. | 5,000 m. 16,404 ft.

COUNTIES

A horse race at the Birmingham Turf Club

INDEX

Page numbers that appear in boldface type indicate illustrations.

**A spring festival
at Five Points South
in Birmingham**

Picture Identifications

Front cover: Bellingrath Gardens
Back cover: Arlington Antebellum Home in Birmingham
Pages 2-3: A farm in the Black Belt
Page 6: Sunset over Lake Logan Martin
Pages 8-9: Sipsey Wilderness
Pages 18-19: Montage of Alabama residents
Page 24: An excavation at Mound State Monument at Moundville
Pages 30-31: A nineteenth-century engraving showing field hands picking cotton on the Buena Vista plantation in Clarke County
Pages 40-41: A pig-iron furnace in Birmingham in the 1880s
Pages 52-53: A dam on the Tallapoosa River
Pages 70-71: The State Capitol in Montgomery
Pages 80-81: The Alabama International Motor Speedway in Talladega
Pages 90-91: Bellingrath Gardens
Page 108: Montage showing the state flag, the state tree (southern pine), the state flower (camellia), and the state bird (yellowhammer)

Picture Acknowledgments

H. Armstrong Roberts: © R. Krubner: Front cover, pages 90-91, 105 (bottom left); © R. Tagg: Page 61 (left); © W. Metzen: Pages 61 (right), 105 (bottom right), 124 (right)
Photo Options: © Ed Malles: Pages 2-3, 4, 11, 17, 75 (left), 83 (left), 87 (bottom left), 93, 95 (right), 110, 111; © Lee Isaacs: Pages 6, 87 (top left); © Michael Clemmer: Pages 8-9, 13; © Marsha Perry: Pages 12, 78 (right), 113; © Marc Stein: Page 18 (top left); © Sonja Rieger: Pages 18 (top right), 77 (top left); © Chuck Snow: Pages 18 (bottom left), 119; © Nancy B. Johnson: Page 50; © Ruth Snow: Pages 52-53; © Spider Martin: Pages 74, 85 (left), 117, 141; © Mark Bondarenko: Page 75 (right); © R.P. Falls: Pages 80-81, 83 (right); © Jerry C. Smith: Page 84; © Kenny Walters: Page 85 (right); © Courtland W. Richards: Pages 88, 94, 121, 138; © John McGinn: Page 89 (left); © Helen Kittinger: Page 108 (tree, bird, flowers)
© **Charles Beck Studio:** Pages 5, 78 (left)
© **Dave Hamby:** Pages 14, 23, 77 (bottom left), 79, 105 (top), 106, 114, 125
Root Resources: © Edgar Cheatham: Pages 15, 39; © Mary A. Root: Pages 77 (right), 122; © David Dobbs: Page 87 (bottom right); © William H. Allen, Jr.: Page 101; © Vera Bradshaw: Pages 123, Back cover; © Sylvia Martin: Pages 16, 58
© **Ric Moore:** Pages 18 (bottom right), 19 (all photos), 89 (right), 103, 116, 120
© **Virginia Grimes:** Page 21
Alabama Bureau of Tourism: Pages 24, 99 (right), 107
Mound State Monument: Page 26 (left); © Krebs: Page 26 (right)
Horseshoe Bend National Military Park: Page 29 (both photos)
The Granger Collection, New York: Pages 30-31, 36 (right), 37, 44, 47, 56, 130 (King)
Historical Pictures Service, Inc., Chicago: Pages 33, 34, 36 (left), 38, 40-41, 49, 128 (Carver, Curry), 131 (Wallace), 132
North Wind Picture Archives: Pages 43, 129 (Gorgas)
Wide World Photos: Pages 46, 66, 127 (both photos), 128 (Black, Cole), 129 (Fletcher, Keller, King), 130 (Lee, Mays, Parks), 131 (Sparkman)
UPI/Bettmann: Pages 64, 65 (left), 67, 69
Southern Stock Photos: © Ralph Krubner: Pages 65 (right), 70-71, 99 (left)
Alabama Shakespeare Festival, Montgomery, Alabama: © Phil Scarsbrook: Page 87 (top right)
Photri: Pages 95 (left), 124 (left), 131 (Washington)
© **Frank C. Williams:** Page 97 (left)
© **Jim Taylor:** Pages 97 (right), 98
Marilyn Gartman Agency: © Mark E. Gibson: Page 118
W.S. Hoole Special Collections Library, University of Alabama: Page 131 (Tutwiler)
Len W. Meents: maps on pages 93, 101, 103, 136
Courtesy Flag Research Center, Winchester, Massachusetts 01890: Flag on page 108

About the Author

Sylvia McNair is the author of numerous books for adults and young people about interesting places. A graduate of Oberlin College, she has toured all fifty of the United States and more than thirty foreign countries. Her travels have included many visits to Alabama. Always interested in education, she served for six years on a district school board in Illinois. McNair now lives in Evanston, Illinois. She has three sons, one daughter, and two grandsons.

McNair, Sylvia.
America the beautiful. Alabama / by
Sylvia McNair. -- Chicago : Childrens
Press, c1989.
144 p. : ill. (some col.) ; 25 cm.
Includes index.

Summary: Introduces this southern
state which slopes gently from a hilly
north to the coastal plains along the
Gulf of Mexico.

ISBN 0-516-00447-6

1. Alabama--Juvenile literature. I.
Title II. Title: Alabama